The Hanged Man:

The Story of Ron Van Clief

By

Ron Van Clief and Sparky Parks

ISBN-13: 978-1466374232

ISBN-10: 1466374233

Printed in the United States of America.

Dedication

It has almost taken 70 years to write this book. My mother Doris has been the cornerstone of my life. She is the strongest women I have ever met. It is what it is and that's that! She only had two children; Pete and I were born 1943 and 1944 respectively. Her love and strength has made me what I am today. My father, Allaire 'Larry' taught me rage and fear! My brother Larry 'Pete' who was killed in Vietnam in 1966 at the age of 22, taught me to never give up. Pete was my hero.

My bodybuilding and fitness mentors; Mr. Kenny Hall, Mr. Dan Lurie, and Mr. Joe Bonomo gave me the thirst for physical perfection. The first step in my over 50 year martial arts' journey started in Brooklyn, New York. Grandmaster Moses Powell trained me in the art of Sanuces jiu-jitsu in the 1950's. He was a master at defying gravity and control with biomechanical artistry. Truly amazing self defense. Grandmaster Peter G. Urban taught me Aiki jitsu and Zenpsychotherapy. He taught that martial arts were 90% mental and 10% physical. Grandmaster Ronald Duncan, Ninjitsu pioneer, gave me the spirit of the ninja. Grandmaster S. Henry Cho taught me the essence of Tae Kwon Do. Grandmasters Frank Ruiz, Harry Rosenstein, Chuck Merriman and Ronald Taganashi taught me the essence of competition fighting, kata and self defense. Grandmaster Bruce Lee named me 'BLACK DRAGON' at the All-American Championship at Madison Square Garden in New York City. Grandmasters Leung Ting, Remy Presas, Leo Fong, Fukai Yang and Duncan Leung shared their secrets of oriental fighting arts with a young 'Hak Gwai' called the Black Dragon. Grandmaster Carter Wong my gung fu brother, a veteran of over 100 kung fu movies when I met him in 1973. We became gung fu brothers in Thailand on the set of 'Way of the Black Dragon' which the Ron Van Clief Company debuted at the Negro Ensemble Company in NYC. *The Tiger and the Dragon* was a three act play, a live kung fu movie on stage at the Robert F. Kennedy Theater on Broadway. My kung fu brother, Grandmaster Owen Watson and I performed many choreographed sequences with weapons, lighting, music and sound effects. He believed he was a kung fu master of ancient times. There will never be another Owen Watson. To the teachers who follow the path of Chinese Goju thank you. Arnold LaCruise, Danny Witherspoon, Courtney Faison, Jaime Milnes, Marco Ovalle, Tom Daly, Jeffrey Craig, Glenroy Warrington, Kan Kan Seku, Radu Teodorescu, Thomas Richard Joiner, Tavis DeWindt, Sidney George, Ralph Vicini, Tom Felder, Kevin and Dana Schatzle, Michael Carro, Ade Warrington, April Lui, Taimak and Janet Bloem. My black belt students and Kai's godfathers, Robert Halmi Jr. and Rick Aidekman who changed my life with their genuine friendship and dedication. Radu Teodorescu for teaching me the art of personal training. My friends and family Ms. Lee Wade, Iron Mike Tyson, David Scott Klein, Duane G. Sweet, Rory Calhoun, Paul Schneider, Maybank Scurry, Finlay Townsend, Robert Williams, Hui Cambrelen, David Claudio, Tayari Casel, Gary Catus, William Sessums, Felipe Luciano, Gerald Singer, Eddie Dixon, Hector Martinez, Alina Niculae, Mariana Gross, Gabi and Neptina Moraru and Razvan and Luci Prohor for their enduring friendship. Thank you.

Music icon and guitar genius Mr. George Benson for his spiritual guidance and patience. Movie icon Samuel L. Jackson for his 'reality thinking'. Spike Lee for his cinematic excellence and for keeping it real. Melvin Van Peebles my hero and mentor. Michael Schultz for his passion and professionalism. Action superstar Wesley Snipes for his strength of conviction. Mr. William Heft who inspired me to become a member of the BOYS' HIGH SCHOOL LEADER CORPS honing my horizontal bar, trampoline, rings and freeform floor gymnastics routines. Commander Vaughn of the Blue Jackets taught military strategy and tactics to me as a teenager. My United States Marine Corps Parris Island Marine Recruit Depot Drill Instructors: Sgt. Smokey Stover, Sgt. McCall and Sgt. Norton; thanks for the inspiration and dedication to duty. You took civilian shit and turned Platoon 1003 into professional killing machines. OORAH Semper Fi!

My wife Simina, for putting up with me for 12 years. She is one hell of a woman. I love her very much. My son Ron Jr. aka 'Shihan' for being the best son anyone could ever have. My son, Kai for giving me new life. My grandchildren Aolani and Sy I love you both very much. Thank you Ralph Vicini, my brother from another mother for the love and dedication. Love and respect to my brother Lance 'Sparky' Parks for making my story happen. Thank you to my editor Debbie Lindgren for breathing life into the manuscript. Rene Carter, my brother, a filmmaker, photographer and graphic artist that designed this book cover.

Thanks to my brothers in my 2011 graduation class at Lyons New Jersey Veterans Hospital Combat PTSD Program. We all share the same pain; Sonny Sabine, Big John Holcombe, Sultan Rasool Ali, Joe Quigley, Ron Brooks, Tom Dyson, Byron Rodney, Dave Kovac, Horace Brown, John Fitzpatrick, Mike Carro, Jimmy Wayman, Kevin Bisset, John E Gardner, Jack Biodulph, Tony Vetusche and Jim Paliani. Special thanks to Dr. Terrence Killebrew, Sharon Morrison, Joe Vernic and 'Doc' Walter Bridgers for bringing me back to life. There is life after death. To the staff at Lyons PTSD; especially the ladies at the front desk Stephanie, Cathy, Vivian, Patty and Ms. Evelyn - thank you for your professionalism, dedication and kindness. You turned my 45 day stay at Lyons PTSD into a life lesson. Something I will never forget. Finally, to all my friends and enemies that unknowingly contributed to my positive outlook on life, love and friendship. Thank you!

The Black Kung Fu Experience, *BlackDragon: The Legend of Ron Van Clief* and *Boulevard Warriors* are three documentaries in which I am featured and are due out in 2012. I hope you enjoy them and this book.

The Hanged Man

Chapter 1

Ron Van Clief with his mother Doris

The sticky humidity of the Carolinas pasted their fatigues to their bodies and left them sleek like a leopard's spots in the moonlight. Floods of hatred sounded through the south louder than the bellow of bullfrogs on the 4th of July, tearing apart more of the nation's fabric than a tornado or a hurricane. In the height of segregation anybody darker than cotton was of menial equivalence. Signs read 'Whites Only' on the windows of store fronts. There were signs on the outsides of public restrooms forbidding Negros to enter, with an arrow pointing them to a dirty shack across the street infested with litter and shit. The defecation was so overwhelmingly putrid; a man lost his dignity when he resurfaced from the depths of the bog.

Man can only run so far away until he finds himself hitting the same brick wall. Ron was a Marine in boot camp. In three months he would leave North Carolina retuning home a hero and then set off to travel the world. He'd made it through the most grueling rituals and only claimed his manhood. He'd been forced from his virginity because virgins have something to live for and whores don't.

She was plump and black and sweet enough to arouse, which was her job to do. Her hair was in copper braids and her skin was a brushed caramel candy color. She smelled like barbershop tonic. Her breath reeked of cigarettes. She held him in her arms and he closed his eyes as she felt him harden and took him into the darkness. And then it was over and the whore laughed to herself under her breath as the young man before her found the pieces of his stained uniform to put back on in bewilderment.

"Do I pay now?" he asked.

"No, your friends paid for you," she teased, counting the stack of bills. She smiled and threw back her hair giving him her eyes. "You can come back if you want to practice again. I'll give you half price."

"I'll think about it," he said, lying through the guilt he felt in his heart and the overwhelming pleasure he could not explain.

He left the brothel and walked the road through the darkness past the Negro shacks in the swamp until he was into the small town where he could take the bus back to base. The frogs croaked and the crickets sang their high pitched opera through the humidity. The mosquitoes were sticky on his neck, relentless for blood. The Marine Corp left his mind and he thought of Brooklyn in the summertime playing in the streets as the boy he once used to be and sitting at the table with his mother and father for supper. They were smiling and he couldn't remember that thought, because he placed it there by accident to make believe his beatings weren't for nothing.

Ron walked the empty streets of the town under the glow of the buzzing street lights. He stood on the corner and waited for the bus. A truckload of young white kids drove by throwing bottles at his feet. Reality came back. He was a Private First Class in the United States Marine Corp. He was a trained killer. His senses perked up as he made eyes with a pretty girl across the street, now reliving all the thoughts from his moments just before and wanting to know how to handle them from now on.

When the bus came, he paid his fare and took a seat. There were only a dozen people and he found a seat by himself in the third row back. He stretched his feet out, gazing beyond the window to the countryside, passing in the shadows beneath the light of the moon.

A soda can hit him in the back of the head and he turned to several drunken college boys.

"Get in the back *Nigger*," they taunted.

Ron's neck grew hair.

"I ain't a *nigger*," he said coldly. "I'm a Marine and I'll sit where I want to, thank you."

"You ain't shit and you ain't sittin' on my bus you fucking coon," replied the oldest of the boys coming with a closed fist into Ron's blind spot. Ron felt him approach and ducked as the fist grazed the back of his head. He grabbed the boy by his wrist and hyper extended the boy's elbow with a precise blow on the back of his arm. The rest of them pounced. They were around the same age as Ron. The difference was Ron had been trained to kill men in hand to hand combat. He was no longer a boy and he would not be treated like an animal. They pounded him with fists and he would not let them take him to the ground. Ron broke several noses and gave them an equal beating. The bus driver called over his radio and took a detour towards the police station stopping in front of the jail. The police mobbed the bus and tore them from each other. Ron spent the night on a bed of concrete.

He sat in the jail cell built for black people. The Negroes looked him up and down. He could tell from the way they spoke they probably couldn't read or write. It wasn't their fault. The blacks in the south were essentially forbidden to read books and teachers wouldn't have them in their schools. Their crimes were petty but their punishments beat the alternative of a lynch mob. One had stolen a chicken and another boy was beaten so badly his eye was swollen shut where his jaw was broken into the eye socket. This one did not speak and waited for the rest of the boys to bring him water and wipe the blood from his lips as he choked to swallow it down.

"Did you miss curfew?" One asked.

Blacks were hunted in the dark in pickup trucks with spotlights. They were cornered and taken; sometimes to be dragged behind the trucks down the county dirt roads. Others were beaten and left for dead. The Ku Klux Klan was a fearsome menace at this time. Ron listened to the other boys' stories of horror while holding himself together. He'd been broken down by dead generals and built back up as a Marine. Fear was not an alternative. Survival was the only option. At sunset on the next day, Ron was released.

4

He walked out of town in the direction of the base hoping to hitch a ride. He'd be in hot water now for missing bunk call and probably beaten by the drill instructors. He turned the corner down the main road that was lit by only one street lamp. He heard the rumble of a motor vehicle and tires spitting rocks.

A horn went hysterical and headlights shined in his eyes. An old Ford truck barreled down upon him and then he was surrounded in the streets and they beat him with bats and shovels. They came from the darkness with torches blazing; twenty or more of them with white masks covering their faces. They screamed and hollered; their breaths riling with the stench of drink. They kicked him with the heels and toes of their boots. They punched him with their fists. They spit on him and they cursed him but he did not give up. He was seized from behind by the neck with a noose. His face was taut in the last hopes of triumph over terror when he looked down to see the tattoo of a globe and an anchor on the forearm of the man choking tighter around his neck. He struggled as long as he could until the lights disappeared and he stopped breathing.

The rope held his limp head pivoted on his shoulders and was tightened once more when they hoisted his dead weight from the ground. His face was mangled and blood gleamed from the light reflecting on his face as he twirled and they stretched him. The rope pulled his neck against the weight of his body until it collapsed and only a crooked eye could see the light. God did not come and the devil said nothing as the Marine and the group of Klan members spun his body around taking turns with the shovel on the African piñata.

"Doctor, this one's bad," called the nurse.

"Oh Jesus! Why don't they just throw these things in the ditches when they find them? It's just taking money away from the people that really need it. I don't have time to deal with this right now."

5

Ron could not see through the bandages around his eyes and head and nodded in and out of consciousness. The doctors had him filled with morphine so the rest of the patients wouldn't have to listen to him moaning. The beating he'd taken broke more than twenty bones in his body. He'd been hanging in the tree until early morning when the lynch mob vanished and out of the darkness came the Negroes from the swamp to cut him down. He was still breathing when they put him on the ground, but his pulse was weak and he would die if they did not get him to the hospital.

"Send his ass to Vietnam with the rest of them" said the doctor upon examining his clipboard. "We'll let the gooks get him. Round up all of them before it goes to hell in a hand basket. Our boys shouldn't be dying out there when we could just send over the *niggers* and be done with it once and for all."

Ron's head popped and he went blank into a coma. When he woke up again, he heard the nurses say, "How much longer will he have to stay here? We don't want that *nigger* in our hospital. It isn't right. It isn't decent for our sick boys to be subjected to this filthy creature."

"He is the property of the United States Marine Corp," Danny said.

"Then you take him," scorned the doctor.

"How can you be so cruel?"

"Why do you care about this thing Son?" said the doctor pointing at Ron immobilized and floating in and out of consciousness. "Don't you know better? These people shouldn't be here. They're dirty. This hospital is for white people. These things carry diseases. I can't have this Negro contaminating my entire ward. It's a health hazard."

6

"He can't move," Danny cursed them. "How am I supposed to get him out of here when every bone in his body is busted up and broken?"

"I thought you said he was the property of the Marine Corp. Surely the Marines know how to dispose of such inconveniences," finished the doctor impatiently walking away, clearly frustrated with Danny's ignorance.

The sun shone through stained glass windows lighting up a kaleidoscope over the rows of metal frames and mattresses in the grand room of the hospital.

"Hang on Ron," Danny said. "It's going to be ok."

Ron and Danny were best friends. Danny's parents were Italian. They ran a butchery in the city of Chicago. Danny had kindhearted eyes and he didn't care that Ron was black. Danny's own father instilled in him the virtues of colorblindness. Danny did not see a black man or a white man. He saw a human being. He'd grown up on the streets and knew black kids from his neighborhood. It was a more common scene. Neither he nor Ron were accustomed to the festering racism throughout the rural countryside.

"Am I gonna make it?" Ron whispered as he spit out some blood through his broken jaw. Ron tried to laugh under his purple face, wrapped with gauze so that he could not see, but only hear the hate the hospital staff seethed.

"At least you can still drink through a straw, right?"

"Danny, they're going to kill me. I know it."

"If Smokey didn't kill you, I don't think anyone can."

"That mother fucker left me in here to die."

"He's a real piece of work isn't he?"

"Does he know I'm here?"

"Sarge? Sure, the whole base knows you're here. It's probably one of their sick, fucked up ideas to see how you'll deal with the situation. They figure if you make it through all of this they didn't make a mistake giving you First Class."

"Those bastards," Ron tore out beneath the sheets, stretching his blinded gaze as far as it could go outside of the hospital. "I heard them talking."

"They're not serious."

"These racist mother fuckers? Doesn't this look serious Danny?" Ron asked sympathetically philosophic, black and blue beneath bloody bandages.

It was true. They'd all been talking. The doctors and the nurses would discuss the overdoses of intravenous drugs they were going to stick in his I.V. and what forms of myocardial infarction or subdural hematomas they could write on his chart for the records when they forged his autopsy. His body would never make it before a proper examining authority. The small town in North Carolina wouldn't waste the money. He'd be lucky to get a body bag back to Brooklyn and a box of ashes above his mother's sink by the window in the kitchen to look out over every day for the rest of her tortured life.

Ron recovered in the hospital enough to sit up and feed himself with his arms in casts. The other patients heckled him as he lie in his bed restrained like a rabid dog and prodded him with burrs of viral hatred. They only succeeded in confirming his only philosophy of survival; kill or be killed. He closed his eyes and watched them come for him and in his own imagination he clawed at their eyes and ripped out their throats, leaving their genitalia strewn as tapestral adoration for the ball of ignoramus.

The youngsters never stopped talking; never stopped creating ways to reference his existence; never stopped searching for means to cause him aggravation; never stopped to listen to the hatred they dispelled. An elder pop spat on the floor at him from across the room as he crossed his arms and sucked off his bottom lip.

"We're going to kill you spook. You're going to die," they whispered. "Gonna set the dogs on ya."

"You hanged me. You beat me. Your pussies," he'd say. And he was right. Since he'd awakened in rebirth, he could not be touched. The boys would not come within five feet of him for fear they would vanish somehow into a deep bog of voodoo and witchcraft. They would only sit at a distance and like drunken parrots on a ship of cowards, repeat the flick and the fodder echoing in their little fragmented brains.

"Hey *nigger* lover," they yelled as Danny walked in and sat at the edge of Ron's bed. "You's a fag too, Jew!" they cursed.

Tears welled up and drowned Danny's eyes and he fought them back staring into Ron's eyes as they chased the end.

"Listen, I'll get you outta here. There's only enough time before the dawn," he whispered. "Run rabbit. Get some! Remember when they made us run around the yard with our footlockers in our arms, because I got caught sleeping on guard duty and you took the blame. They knew you didn't do it. They didn't care. They made us run around that yard for two weeks straight it seemed, day and night and we puked our guts out constantly and they'd feed us again so we'd have something more to puke up. Run rabbits. That's what we are."

"When can I get out of here?"

"Soon, I can't take you now. They wouldn't let me if I tried. But I'll get you out of here, away from these sons of whores."

"It's rotten buddy."

A hospital orderly came by and furled his lip shooting his fat pink eyes behind his slicked red duck tail.

"Getcha, getcha, getcha," he said.

"Yah get outta here soon, so I can whoop your ass," Danny said as he stood walking away.

"I'll take care of that little prick right now," Ron said, "I only need a finger."

"Hey Jew boy, take your porch monkey with you," they taunted. "Don't take too long or you'll be cutting him down from the rafters again when you get back."

Chapter 2

Pete and Ron Van Clief

The year was 1960. Ron stood in the middle of Times Square facing the Marine Corps Recruiting Station. The clock said ten to two. He chewed on his lip and squeezed his palms open and closed deliberating his decision for a minute before he finally sucked up his breath and opened the door. Standing before him was the tallest white man he'd ever seen. He had a chiseled jaw line, broad shoulders, arms as long as Ron's legs and just as thick. He was identical to the man on the poster for the Marine Corp commercials: dress blues, white gloves and hat, the gold handled sword in his scabbard and medals on his chest. There was a purple heart and a cross of some sort as well as the ribbons, bands and stripes hanging from his shoulders and arms. Ron was in awe. He knew only that the decorations were important. The man moved and startled Ron as though he'd been a statue frozen in glory.

"Good day Son," said the man with the deepest voice Ron had ever heard. He extended his hand to shake Ron's. Ron saw the big white hand coming towards him and time froze. The man had a grip like Moses Powell, capable of breaking his body with the touch of a finger. Ron could feel the man would be able to accomplish such a task with ease and he surrendered finally in the space of time by shaking the man's hand and looking him in the eye.

"Pleasure to meet you," he spoke up. "Ron Van Clief."

"Lieutenant James McDonald of the Third Battalion, United States Marine Corp," said the man.

There wasn't a spot on the Marines' uniform. He was clean shaven and perfect. Ron immediately began to emulate by falling under the rhetoric and influence of the senior recruiting officer. He sat across from the lieutenant in a wooden chair wrapped in cherry red leather. Pictures adorned the wall of battles in France, Germany, Poland and everywhere else the Marines had conquered and left alone again for freedom to rekindle its valiant flame.

Directly behind the recruiting officer was a giant picture of the John Wayne classic, *The Sands of Iwo Jima*, with that historic image of the Marines raising the flag after so many hours and days of losing life and taking so much of it to leave forever set in stone that no enemy has ever since known a greater and more formidable opponent. The poster, the pictures and the giant white man melded a world inside Ron's adolescent mind. The heroics and the adventures of the Marine Corp captivated him more than all the comic books he'd read. This was a chance to be the real Captain America.

Intimidation and awe would rip Ron from Brooklyn's Lower East Side and the pathetic rags children could find to survive. He would take out the trash so to speak; eradicate the spawn of negligent whores refuging Indian reservations. Senior Van Clief leaving them flinging spun out on the rot and left to life on the side of the road on his way with his cavalry. The Marines didn't care if you were half black, half Indian a quarter white or quarter anything. All men bleed red. In a world where men were made, Ron wanted to be one of them and he went home to tell his family about this new world and was ready to leave behind the filth and struggle of inner city life.

Ron was only 17. He had not yet finished high school and was too young to enlist but it did not matter. The days had passed until he could stand it no longer. He wanted more than anything to be a Marine. They were the toughest warriors he'd ever seen and their stories of bravery and heroism spanned the globe. They went into battle leaving their emotions at home. They fought for freedom and claimed only flagpoles as their conquering emblems and took only enough land to bury the men it took to ensure such liberties.

Ron needed the consent of his parents. He was terrified of his father Allaire. Allaire was a drug addict with a bad temper and a mind overwrought with horrible memories of the past. With the words of the lieutenant echoing in his mind and the hopes of becoming a real American hero, Ron began the long walk home to beg permission.

Allaire Van Clief was a tall man. He stood six foot three inches, towering over Ron at only five foot nine. Allaire Van Clief was a professional boxer in the Bronx in the early 1920's where gloves were just a layer of cowhide wrapped up in string. There were no mouth pieces, only the wooden teeth a fighter pulled when he spit in the bucket upon entering the ring. Allaire had given and taken more lickings than the next man twice his swagger.

Allaire had left home to find work at an early age by joining the Merchant Marines. He was the only black man, a cook on a boat with thirty men. His scars of prejudice were layered so thickly upon him he did not care about killing men with his bare hands should he speak out of disrespect or reference to the color of his skin. Life hated him and he hated life back because he was nothing in the world worth anything

13

and as far as he was concerned his Ron was worth even less. He didn't want a fairy and when Ron had mildly entertained the idea of enlisting in the armed forces, he caught such a cold icy stare from his father that he knew one day that stare would turn into a violent rage.

Allaire wanted his son to stay in the world of reality, always scolding him for being too lofty in his thoughts and wasting time dancing in front of the mirror practicing his 'karate'. Ron in turn wanted more than anything to impress his father. He tried to love his father even when Allaire was so drunk he would black out and not remember beating Ron the night before.

Ron feared and respected his father. He enjoyed watching his father's enormous hands with a pencil on paper, drawing the pictures he himself could never master and though these drawings inspired Ron to draw more, he was met with cruelty by Allaire when he was caught wasting his time with such 'worthless' causes. By the age of six Ron could draw any cartoon from memory. He fell in love with writers and poets and would stay up late drawing and painting by the light of the candle.

When Ron told his father he was going to enlist in the Marine Corp, Allaire threw him across the room and then breaking a chair over Ron's face, stumbled from the room and out the door. Ron lie on the floor knocked out cold from the chair hitting his temple. When he woke his father was gone. Later when Allaire came home drunk, Ron was beaten some more.

Doris sympathized with her eldest son. What could a mother do? She pleaded for days that Ron stop his foolishness and come to his senses and not to go off to fight and learn how to kill. Doris did not consult with her husband and in the end she did what she felt was the right thing to do for her son and signed the permission papers behind Allaire's back, allowing Ron to enlist in the Marines.

Ron went back to the Marine Corp Recruiting office in Times Square and put his mother's signature on the desk in front of the recruiting officer. At that moment the shy young teenager would be taken on a ride further and further from the adolescent young mind to begin the reprogramming of his brain; reconfiguring the embryonic coding of a professional killer and psychopathic assassin.

Chapter 3

Ron's parents, Allaire and Doris Van Clief

The Van Clief's were poor. They lived in an old rail car turned into a flat which was in a row of flats upon rows of flats. Sara Pitts lived in the flat next door with his cousins Kirk, Boo, Ham and Horace. Horace joined the Marine Corps when Ron was 15 and at that time Ron set that goal for himself. When Ron started training at the age of 12, he made his first set of weights out of paint cans filled with cement. He built his own gym in the backyard with pull up bars and kicking stumps. He tied ropes to bricks and curled them up with his biceps. He found an old rug and practiced his Jiu Jitsu on his brother Pete and his cousin Kirk. They always hit him with no regard for technique but rather to inflict as much pain on their smaller kin as possible. As much as they beat him, Ron would not cry or return the anger the two seemed to feel inside. He learned at a young age to compose himself under tight situations, strangled of breath and beaten until his opponent's exhaustion gave him a moment to gain an advantage, allowing him to submit larger aggressors.

In those days tenements had large backyards between neighboring buildings. Tenants on the upper floors strung lines between the buildings to hang clothes on. It was a zigzag of spider webs colored with garments like flowers on a concrete vine. From the kitchen window in the railcar flat, Ron could see beyond the backyard to the playing field of Junior High School 178. They would climb up the side of the building like ninjas. They used no tools except their hands and feet, climbing five stories up between two buildings.

He used his hands to support himself as he raised his legs higher. They looked like spiders scaling the building walls while calling out to each other scenes from the Spiderman comic books.

Ron began martial arts training and that along with his drawing and painting were his real passions. His mother Doris encouraged him to be an artist and painter of the renaissance and he learned to step outside the scope of constructed thinking into an abstract world. He loved to draw landscapes, cartoons and comic books. She encouraged him in everything he wanted to do and told him he could be whatever he wanted to be. Ron went to Boys' school in Brooklyn.

Kirk's mom worked the graveyard shift at the hospital and didn't get home until 8:30 in the morning on the D day train that ran through the city. She worked long hours and eventually they were able to afford the luxuries of a two bedroom apartment in the Lower East Side. Kirk was two years older than Ron. He was a terrifying individual by the age of 16.

When Ron was fifteen years old, he fell out Aunt Sarah's kitchen window. He leaned back on a windowsill to support his back on the frame. The window was open so Ron missed the window frame and fell backwards five stories to the ground. Luckily the hanging laundry lines broke his fall. At one moment, he was talking to his cousins and laughing about a joke that Kirk told, and then suddenly he was flying backwards down through the laundry ropes and branches. He looked up from the fall to the window and saw his mother staring back down. His cousins surrounded him until the ambulance came and took him to the hospital where he needed 15 stitches.

Kirk shared a room with his sister June, but when he had company which was almost every night, he went into his mother's room and locked the door. Ron would pick him up on the way to the bus or train every morning ever since Ron started kindergarten. Kirk would usually still be asleep, having passed out in the early hours of the morning with one of his girlfriends from the night before. Ron would shake him awake and then make some Ovaltine while whoever's sister got dressed and came out of the bedroom in a tarnish of her own dishevelry. June was terrified to say anything. Kirk would light up a cigarette first thing in the morning, a habit he started when he was twelve, rinse it down with a rich chocolaty beverage and the two of them were out the door. After Ron and Kirk left the house, June would make up the bed and clean the room before her mother got home so she could have her rest without worry or concern. June was a wizard with numbers. She had tutored Ron with his math homework when he went to Boys' High so that he could pass his classes.

Kirk was the fearless leader. He took Ron on adventures making him test everything first. He was a bully and made Ron do whatever he demanded. They were the best of friends but Kirk had an evil streak in him. Kirk would always lock Ron in the bathroom with his dog Silver. Silver was a little white terrier; a ferocious monster. He'd been trained to attack anybody who came too close to Kirk. Ron loved dogs but

Silver didn't like anybody but Kirk. One day they came home from school and no one was there. Kirk went to the refrigerator for a sandwich and juice and Silver found his chance to attack Ron.

Ron wanted so much to be the dog's friend. Kirk reminded him time and time again not to touch Silver, but Ron was stubborn and did not listen. He reached out to pet the dog and Silver jumped for Ron's throat and pinned him to the ground biting Ron on his arm and chest. Kirk laughed for a few minutes while the dog frothed at the mouth biting open flesh, drawing the crimson punctures open with its razor sharp teeth. After a few moments of screaming Kirk pulled the dog away smiling and said, "I told you so."

"What the hell?"

"Don't cuss."

"Screw you," Ron said and Kirk laughed smacking him upside the head with a backhand.

"Where's your manners?"

"You're such an asshole."

"You know you love me."

"I don't."

"Well then, leave."

The relationship was unconditional. Ron was rather shy and reserved. He was quiet and kept to himself. He looked up to his cousin as a role model who replaced the absence of his drunk and addicted father. When Ron was tired of taking a beating, it was Kirk who opened the door for him to the world of martial arts.

Kirk collected weapons; knives, throwing stars, swords and as he grew older, guns. Weapons in the hands of children often times baffles the minds of society which bears witness to tragic horrors committed on grown adults. The terror involved left mothers staying up late night holding back tears in front of their babies making a promise for a safer world. Ron would learn to use these weapons and to defend against them.

Kids on the Lower East Side had no choice but to be ferocious or be eaten by the ferocity of ghetto bastards. Jose Cordero was Ron's first Puerto Rican friend. Jose was brilliant with an IQ around 160 and had his own business by the age of 13. He had a collection of the newest comic books from the 1950's and the old ones on yellow newsprint. He was so meticulous that all of the comic books were catalogued in a file cabinet alphabetically, by year and genre. He had thousands of comic books. He had the golden touch and made money before he was ten. He did things like picking up newspapers he found on the ground from the morning rush, tidying them up and then selling them for pure profit. The business became so lucrative that he started missing school. In order to stay in school, because he loved it, he started buying used comic books in bulk from the suppliers and selling them after school in the park. Kids skipped lunch so they could buy comic books from Jose.

His parents were out of the picture and with no parental control or authority to keep him in line; he invested his profits and built up his revenues. With more money came the ability to buy more expensive luxury items. Because Brooklyn was a tough neighborhood, Jose invested his money in arms. He became a warlord at the age of fifteen for the most notorious Puerto Rican gang in Williamsburg at the time.

He was the scariest kind of kid. He was short and stocky and could put his fist through a wall. Jose, Kirk and Ron would swim in the East River. They would jump off the pier into the bay where the big freight transport ships docked. The drop depended on the tide and where they jumped so they could maximize the distance to the water without the fear of falling at a longer rate of time. They swam out between the columns of the pier underneath the walkway to a secret hideout in the rocky walls of the harbor.

Jose had built a small fortress impenetrable from above and only reachable by water. Jose built this small shack by fastening timbers to the planks of the pier. He used tarpaulins on the ceiling and the walls to protect it from the elements. He had a small canoe which he used to transport building supplies covertly at night. He had cigarettes and food rations, candles, blankets, fresh water; everything he needed to survive for weeks at a time in case he needed to hide from rival gang members.

Ron and Kirk would ride their bicycles to Williamsburg several blocks from Jose's house. Jose would take them to the secret spots within the gang's territory outlining the boundaries for other gangs to stay away. Ron met everybody in the gang. They dealt drugs and prostitution. Ron was oblivious to such things at the time and did not understand until much later the struggle with the evil medicines his father injected himself with. He did not see women as hookers because he had never thought about having sex before. Though Ron's mind was artistic, his body had not yet crossed the threshold of puberty inspiring the thousands of thoughts a boy thinks about a woman throughout the hours of every day.

His senior year he fell in love with Jose's sister Carmen. She was the closest thing Ron ever had to a girlfriend. They were both 17 years now and knew nothing about life but that they wanted to see the world. Ron believed he would see the world in the Marine Corps. Carmen encouraged Ron in his dream. They were in love and didn't know any better.

Ron finished his senior year. All summer he prepared for the Marine Corp at Parris Island. He trained as hard as he'd ever trained in his life. He, his cousin Kirk and Jose all trained with Ronald Duncan, the professor of Nin Jitsu.   Ron could now do 300 pushups and 250 dips repetitiously. He would work out with Duncan in the morning, practice Sanuces Ryu Jiu Jitsu with Master Moses Powell in the afternoon and then train Shotokan Karate with George Cofield and Tom LaPuppet before going to train again at Peter Urban's dojo in Chinatown at night where he learned Goju Ryu Karate. All of them were ex-military guys who brought martial arts back from overseas. The combination of techniques made the boys unbeatable opponents on the street.

One day Jose and Ron were leaving the metropolitan pool. They found themselves suddenly surrounded by ten gang members from a rival gang. One of them was holding a shot-gun on Ron.

"Hey Spooky, where do you think you're going?"

Ron did not move. "Home I suppose."

"You suppose? Well just suppose you get your two asses shot in the face."

The rest of the gang members laughed. Jose quickly be-came aggravated and with the stealth of a striking snake he jumped between Ron and the shotgun grabbing the barrel, holding it to his head between his eyes and smiling.

"You want to kill me?" he shouted. "You want to fucking kill *me*?" he screamed. "Go ahead. If you can pull the trigger then play God. See if you have what it takes you chicken shit mother fucker."

At that moment the boy with the gun against Jose's head clicked off the safety. Jose yanked the shotgun passed his head as the blast from the primer exploded in his ears and everything became slow motion.

Ron kicked two of the gang members in the face with circular kicks. Jose was all over the guy with the shotgun. He picked up the shotgun and fired at the gang members. Jose clipped the attacker on the elbow of his right arm blowing half of it away. He screamed and straggled off. The rest of the gang scattered.

"Punks," Jose spit on the ground. "Run like the cowards you are, sons of whores," he said exchanging the remaining shells from the magazine. "That's the problem with gangs," he said staring down the street as if he were on the dawn of a new frontier atop a horse with a wide brimmed hat around his brow, looking at the distance as the spit gets dryer and the mouth chokes on the blade of grass it's been chewing for the last fifty miles. "They have no heart. They're just a bunch of cowards who will grow up to be a terrible burden on our society."

Later that summer Jose was arrested for carrying a gun and shooting another gang member. He faced twenty years to life but because they did not try him as an adult, the lawyer made a plea bargain for information on the rival gang's activities. Jose went away to a reform school ruining his chances to enlist in the Marine Corp. Jose and Ron had planned to go into the Corps after graduating that summer from Boys' High School but Jose would never get the chance. The reform school made him even more rebellious and when he got out he dove deeply into the Puerto Rican gang world. He smoked pot and started doing coke and heroin. He became a crackhead and lost everything, sometimes wandering along the streets looking into trash cans finding tin cans to rip the labels off, putting them inside the can and then inside the garbage again. His girlfriend panicked at the thought of being poor again and jumped from the fifth story kitchen window breaking her neck and eventually dying in the hospital.

Chapter 4

Ron Van Clief at age 17

Ron's mind lived inside the movie theaters, watching cowboy and war movies in Brooklyn off the corner of Saratoga Avenue and Dean Street where they played John Wayne movies, that shaped him for his life ahead. He wanted to be the black cowboy riding off into the sunset as the hero. He watched the westerns over and over; Bonanza, Gunsmoke and Rawhide. He lived them; tipping his straw hat in the mirror while practicing his quick draw and saying, "Howdy Pilgrim."

But that summer of 1960 was a circus passing ever so quickly and before long Ron was standing in Penn Station along with hundreds of other dazed recruits. The new recruits were packed onto train cars like cattle; with total disdain for dignity.

All the recruits were scared regardless of what they said. They looked around for something familiar hoping they'd made the right decision. They had found fear for the first time; the same fear their mothers experienced as they sat home holding back the pain with prayers that their babies come home safe off the streets. The boys still laughed and made jokes.

"Get a load of this guy."

"I can't believe they let in coloreds."

"If this is going to be some kind of diversity training seminar then I'm out of here."

"Keep it moving," someone in green barked out.

"All aboard for bus 1-9!" blasted out another voice over the loud speaker. Everyone wanted to be somewhere else except that train. Ron took no regard to their comments. Where he was going racism didn't exist. How could it? He could see it now. They would put them all in a machine and they would all come out the same color covered in green with eyes commanding respect in every gaze. There was no racism in the dojo. There couldn't be racism in the Marines.

The new recruits watched the passing countryside from the windows as the train rolled through the Carolinas. Ron let his mind travel to the ends of the earth. He said goodbye to his family, his brother Pete and his cousin Kirk. Goodbye to the city and the Lower East Side. He kissed his mother and smiled and told her he loved her.

The Marine Corps would make him a man. The sacrifice would be incredible. He'd heard all the horror stories and read the books. He played soldier in his mind his entire life and trained every day to be ready for this challenge. Finally, he rested his head between the window and the seat and sat back listening to the wheels under the train going around.

When the train arrived in South Carolina the recruits were unloaded and loaded again into five Marine Corps trucks, packed into the back and driven off covered under the dark enclosure of the army canvas. The trucks were going to the receiving station at Parris Island; the factory for building Marines. The ride lasted an eternity, stretching the butterfly's wings over the thread of a thousand stitches; each one sewing up the guts of weakness and any trace that it ever existed. If there were any chuckles and laughter getting on the bus, they were gone now. Nobody spoke. Nobody said a word. The afternoon sun was setting in the west spilling out a hundred colors of fire in the belly of the purple eye of a storm. The breeze lifted, chilling the sweat on their backs as they sat up in their seats when the bus made its last turn down a long dirt road into the hills and through the trees.

The gates of Parris Island opened and the recruits were ushered into the surreal world of boot camp. Their legs froze stiff and their knees wobbled, unable to support their chests and a shortness of breath in the lungs that pounded against their racing hearts.

In the distance on the parade ground was the giant monument of the Marines raising the American flag at Mt. Iwo Jima. Whistles blew and orders were screamed as they filed out in a disorderly fashion onto the grass like a herd of lost sheep. Ron stared up in awe at the monument letting his jaw drop. His eyes lifted to the clouds where he saw John Wayne saluting back down at him with his big hero's smile. His dream had come true. He'd come to the right place. Parris Island was where heroes were manufactured.

The recruits were rounded up in front of a row of wooden barracks known as the receiving station. They were given a physical examination and underwent a battery of classification testing. The basic unit of the Marine Corps was the rifleman infantry learning hand to hand combat. He would become the cornerstone of the fire team. They were asked a series of questions and ordered to do various exercises while men in uniform made notes on clipboards separating them into smaller groups. The nurses gave them shots and the doctors made them cough and grab their Jolly Rogers.

After the tests, the recruits were rushed into an old airplane hangar where they got their heads shaved bald to mirror the synonymous innocence of a psychopath. They were doused with louse powder, because skin heads weren't scary enough and when they finally emerged as naked bald ghosts, they were issued 782 gear; all one needs to be a U.S. Marine. They formed one long line passing in front of bins collecting items wherever they were thrown at them, most of it falling to the floor, warranting an onslaught of vocabulary from an incomprehensible diatribe. If the recruits dropped anything, they were kicked and slapped and pushed out of the way. The punishment for dropping each item was a thousand pushups. They were moving targets for socks, skivvies, boots, shirts, pants and toothbrushes and everything they had when they came in, they had no more.

After the Aryan makeover, the recruits were marched into the mess hall where they were made to stand at attention. Their first command "Ready Seat" was given and they sat down all at once. Ron touched a French fried potato before the order was given to eat. From out of nowhere a drill instructor smacked the back of Ron's head slamming his face into the tray of food, breaking his nose. Everyone stopped eating and there was silence in the mess hall. The recruits froze, remaining seated at attention, not one of them even peeking in Ron's direction.

They were beaten for the most minor insubordinations; untied shoelace, crumbs around their mouths, unpressed shirt collars and dirty fingernails. The yelling was enough but nobody could do anything or say anything about the beatings.

Ron was black that was apparent. There were seven of them out of four hundred. These were not the opponents he knew from the streets in the city. These were redneck white boys who pitched hay all day; eyes of the devil for the blackbirds, seven sitting in a tree. Things were supposed to be different. Instead, it was a social club for men mastering the art of war; target practice.

The base marines cursed the seven blackbirds. They were always referred to as niggers so they wouldn't forget. Every day was worse than the first; running forty hours in the rain with the gun and the eyes for the enemy; instilling terror tactics and psychological warfare against ghosts in the shadows. He bit the bullet and was born again. He let his mind go and succumbed to the brainwashing of the United States Marine Corp.

They were assigned to platoon 1003 in the first Battalion Marine Corps Recruit Depot. When they stopped that night, Ron had his sea bag with all of his new belongings in it. He didn't remember falling asleep and dreamt he was in a far off land flying high above the clouds soaring over snowcapped mountain tops covered with forest. The sun burned through a hole in his sleepless being without feeling to the cold. He dove down into the canyons of the most ravenous cliffs and hangs, cutting back up between the splintery sharp edges of jagged rock. From atop a peak in the topography below he saw an eye the color blue staring back through a triangle in a giant castle morphing on and off a template from an alternate hologram. The triangle pulled him closer to the eye until he saw the reflection of himself and the dragon he was riding.

The sound of a garbage can rolling down the middle of the barracks woke them all. Marine Staff Sergeant Smokey Stover stood in the doorway. He was a veteran of the Korean War. The scuttlebutt was that he received the Congressional Medal of Honor. He was a hero and served his country. He was also a redneck and very proud of it. He descended from a caveman lineage and one of his ancestors came over on the Viking ship with skulls of the victims he'd already killed hanging from his neck. Each stripe was three years. He had four or five. Smoky went in for life with no thought of coming out. All lifers wanted to do was to build warriors.

"I hate *niggers* in my Marine Corps," he screamed when he saw Ron. "*Niggers* and spics, you're on my shit list. Don't need ya, can't feed ya. If you do not cut the grade, I will kill you personally for having undermined my very instinct of letting your inferior breed disrupt my platoon's focus and ability to keep itself alive. When it comes down to it, a Marine is responsible for every man next to him on the battlefield. You will be responsible for the next man to you and so on and since there are a couple of undesirables among you, we will learn sweat techniques. How much more will you hate a person when they are bleeding on you? How much more will you hate a person sweating on you when that person is a coon? You pieces of shit will do whatever I tell you to or I will kill you. You will sweat with these *niggers* until there is no more sweat in any of you. If these Negroes are still black by the time I have finished with this exercise, we will do the sweat exercise again until we have cleaned all of you from your error. You are not here to think. You are not here to make errors. You are here to do whatever the fuck I tell you to do or I will kill you myself. Can I get a hoo hah Drill Sergeant?"

Sergeant Smokey Stover, I'll beat your ass to hell and make you swallow mud with pushups. Destroy the body and wipe the mind psychodrama through complete exhaustion. Everybody breaks and half fall out altogether. Anybody sane enough dropped out the first week. There wasn't a draft yet. Ron got it just as much from the blackbirds as he did from anybody else. He was tiny against the rest of the unit. He fought everybody all the time. They pissed on him and poured dirt and sand down his rifle the night before the 'junk on bunk' inspection. He couldn't clean it in the morning and was almost court martialed because of it. When Staff Sergeant Stover examined the contents and belongings in Ron's foot locker, he flipped Ron's bunk on top of him and beat him unconscious. When Ron regained consciousness he was under his mattress and gear. The inspection was over. He was sent to the motivation platoon for ten days. He woke up in the morning and grabbed his locker box and ran around the yard until he fell down. There was no number of laps to run around the yard. What was important was that you finally fell down. When he stopped, Staff Sergeant Smokey Stover beat Ron with a tent pole until he was unconscious again, now bleeding in the mud and the rain with the chew spit of the Staff Sergeant on his face.

Smokey Stover was six foot four inches and weighed a lean two hundred and forty pounds. He taught hand to hand combat. One day in self-defense class he gave Ron a bayonet and ordered Ron to attack him. Ron struck out and Stover deflected it away, flipping Ron back in the air off the ground and then grabbing hold of his neck in a rear naked choke hold. He choked Ron until he was out cold and fell as a pile of black shit in his arms that he let go spilling onto the ground as he walked away for the next target. Ron could not swallow for a month.

Stover's hand to hand combat was lethal. It lacked grace compared with traditional martial arts, but it got to the point quickly and kept you alive and ready for whatever was next. Stover was a super weapon. He was the essence of everything honorable and terrifying at the same time. Blackbirds became shit birds. Staff Sergeant Norton at five feet ten inches and 240 pounds was a pitbull of a drill instructor. He had evil in his eyes. Stover and Norton penetrated the very souls of recruits with their tyrannical stares. They were lions but twice as tough.

They became a superhuman breed capable of the impossible. Stover and Norton played God and terrorized every young man's dreams; turning every civilian piece of shit into a deadly killing machine. Stover could hit the bull's eye standing at 500 yards with an M-1 as many times as he wanted to. He never missed. He was an Olympic gold medalist.

The M-1 was the rifleman's weapon. They had to qualify with the M-1 to become Marines. They were taught to love their rifles like nothing else. Not pussy nor food mattered more. After sixteen weeks of insanity, one third of the platoon had dropped out. One of the recruits did not qualify with the M-1. His name was Private Attard. He was beaten for hours by the drill instructors the night before the test and when he didn't qualify the next morning they broke his leg by stomping on it with boot heels.

Most of the time Ron was on the drill field without a rifle. The manual of arms was the drill they learned as they marched. It had to be performed exactly the same as the rest of the platoon. The recruits fell in line and learned to stay alive. Hundreds of hours of grisly repetition had changed retards into circus gymnasts on a balancing beam.

In boot camp, to qualify with the M-1 and the 1911A-1 45 cal automatic you need a score of at least 180 points. 200 points qualified you as an expert and the maximum score was 250 points. The day of the rifle qualification, Ron qualified as an expert. Private Attard went into the motivation platoon and by the time he'd recovered from his injuries he too qualified as an expert marksman. He'd lost thirty pounds and was fully adjusted to fit his new Marine Corp mentality.

Ron could disassemble and reassemble his weapon blindfolded within two minutes. The privates were learning to survive under any circumstance. After Ron failed the first junk on the bunk inspection, he did not want to fail another. He spit shined his boots and shoes three to four hours a night, a discipline that would set his focus for the rest of his life. Sometimes he would go into the bathroom after lights out to continue shining his shoes and cleaning his rifle.

His position in the fire team was the M-60 operator. The M-60 was an ominous piece of equipment capable of producing lightning and thunder. Small arms became Ron's obsession and he learned everything he could about the Marine Corps weaponry arsenal. He was noticed for his devotion by the drill instructors and promoted to platoon guide, leading the rest of the platoon in drill formation. This was the number one position in the platoon formation. He was a spit shined starch wearing utility Marine.

But his promotions did not come without folly. He was still a black man in boot camp. He was still hated and cursed at under their breaths as he led them. They fought constantly. Ron unleashed his rage upon them. He'd had enough. He found anger and hatred and gave back to them everything that had been put into him. He was lightning fast and it always took more than three to take him out. He lived with Powell and Urban in his mind and rested his thoughts in the dojo in Chinatown. He mixed his martial arts with hand to hand combat training, setting a standard for those who would try and beat him down. He had been beaten so many times that it didn't leave a mark anymore. There was no more response.

The toughest guys were tough in the ring but the farmer boys from the boondocks had the fire of a Spartan. The Marine Corp made them heroes who were now firing machine guns. They were put on a pedestal.

Danny was Ron's only white friend. Well, it was one thing to be black and another thing to be friends with blacks. The other recruits tortured Danny. They beat him extra bad. Boot camp became a nightmare Danny could never escape, but together they held on and survived. Picked each other back up when they could take no more of the days that nearly killed them all.

One day, four boys from Kentucky held Danny down in the Barracks. 'Johnny Reb', a red headed freckle faced son of the Aryan nation, whose grandfather's grandfathers had been illustrious dishonorables in the Ku Klux Klan, cut Danny's face from his left ear to his right eye through the cheek leaving the teeth and muscles to show. The disfigurement shocked his security and he twitched now when a marine should be steady.

Ron was outraged by this atrocity. There was nobody to tell. There was nobody who would listen. Stover and Norton didn't care. They didn't want *niggers* in the Marine Corp. Ron took the retaliation upon himself. He waited for dark when he heard voices from inside the barracks where the privates from Kentucky lived. He pulled the pin on a concussion grenade and rolled it inside the door underneath the bunks towards the voices. There was a loud explosion and screaming. Ron didn't care. Fuck them.

The goal in boot camp was to stay alive. The first battalion prided its field meet tradition more than life itself. Ron was chosen to represent the platoon in the push-up competition. Staff Sgt. Norton told him, "If you don't win, I'll blow your fucking head off." He pressed the cold steel of the .45 cal automatic to Ron's forehead. Every time any of the drill instructors saw him they would make him drop for pushups. He trained. Thousands of repetitions in the push-up position made him oblivious to numbers.

The Parris Island Confidence Course was a system of obstacles in immense proportions. There were ten different obstacles that made up a mission impossible course. Ron trained on and off duty seven days a week. He would quit at nothing. The drill instructors found pleasure in seeing Ron run through the course.

The final obstacle was the 'slide for life' which was a rope suspended between two towers over water. One had to use their legs and arms to travel over one hundred feet. This obstacle was the last to complete and by the time one reached the 'slide for life' exhaustion had beaten them completely.

The drill instructors from the three battalions bet on their troops. Every recruit was in the same hell. The day of the field meet was rapidly approaching; Ron was training day and night. Every morning he did five hundred pushups before he was allowed to get dressed for chow call. He was ready to defend his country like a samurai warrior. Inside he held Esprit de Corps.

The night before the battalion field meet, all the drill instructors came to visit Ron in the barracks. They woke him up after midnight and took him to the recreation room. The last time Ron had seen the rec room, he'd played pool for a punch in the face and lost two teeth. Tonight he was twisted after one of Staff Sgt. Norton's left hooks in the stomach. When Stover and Norton smiled, he knew he was in big trouble. He was immune to pain.

He was called to attention and took a deep breath to his feet assuming attention with his heels together and thumbs lined up at his side; a position of total vulnerability. The drill instructors surrounded him, then ordered him into the pushup position.

Smokey Stover had a stopwatch in one hand and a .45 automatic in the other. Sgt. Norton nodded and Ron started doing pushups. He pointed the .45 to Ron's temple. Sgt. McCall the other drill instructor watched and counted Ron doing pushups. He was chewing tobacco and spitting it in Ron's face. Ron did pushups until four in the morning.

Later that morning, Ron did 253 pushups in three minutes winning the field meet for the first battalion. He was a hero. Platoon 1003 was still the number one platoon in the first battalion. The Commandant of the Marine Corps was there and shook Ron's hand.

The base went on full alert in preparation for General Shoup's inspection.

General David M. Shoup was the first and only General Ron ever saw in person during his five and a half years in the

Marine Corps. A CG Inspection was where the Commanding General personally inspects the entire base. For two weeks the recruits cleaned the barracks and the campgrounds. The big inspection was exactly three days away.

After the CGI, the final field exercises were a snap. They stood at attention in their barracks for hours. The drill instructors came in to give one final look over before the inspection team. Ron's dress shoes were spit shined showing the reflection of the men in line. Every recruit was at the attention position in front of their bunks.

The inspection team slowly worked their way down towards Ron's bunk. The inspecting officer grabbed each recruits rifle and looked down the barrel. You could hear a pin drop. Suddenly there was a silver star in front of Ron. The star was so intimidating, Ron didn't look into the General's eyes.

Automatically Ron's M-1 jumped into his hands for presentation. The General snatched the weapon from Ron's hands. He looked down the bore and rubbed the linseed oil on the rifle stock. The General smiled and moved down the line to the next recruit. Ron could feel the sweat rolling down his back. Platoon 1003 was the pride of the first battalion.

The next day they accomplished a   twenty   mile force march to Elliot's   Beach. This was the   final   phase   of   the training   at   Parris   Island. Ron received   the   meritorious promotion   to Private First Class and was   out   of   boot   camp.

Chapter 5

Lance Corporal Ron Van Clief
3rd Mar Div 105mm Howitzwer battery

After boot camp at Parris Island, Ron and Danny went to advanced infantry training in Camp Le Jeune, North Carolina. After that, they were sent to Guantanamo Bay with the artillery unit, the final training before marines went overseas. There marines learned about the atomic bomb and biological and chemical warfare. Ron loved the artillery; the guns as well as the shells expunged from their cannons blowing up targets miles away.

36

The bond between Danny and himself grew closer. Parris Island had taught them to kill and now they had the seeds of hatred burning inside of them, especially Ron. The roots grew stronger every day burying their innocence. Danny wasn't liked because he was friends with a black man. The men in uniform could not stand that and called them faggots.

There was one man who Ron liked. He was a spit and polish marine captain, head of his own company. He was a rifleman who inspired Ron to be a good marksman. He had pride. He was a poster marine. He was one of the marines who looked like Smokey Stover and could see the enemy miles away in the bushes on the horizon and smell them in his sleep.

Sergeant Van Guard was a little fat black man who'd been in the service for twenty four years and had four hash marks. He was an alcoholic with a terrible contempt for other Negro servicemen, but he was not a bum. He was a decorated marine from Korea. He'd been beaten his fair share and suffered much ridicule during his service. The Sergeant tormented Danny. He was down on everybody. He was a 'by the book' type marine who knew the uniform military code of justice and read it to you all the time. He was a lifer. He could've gotten out, but he stayed in. He was only an E6 or E7 Staff Sergeant.

He didn't like anybody who was white and he treated Danny like any other 'cracker head mother fucker' from Tennessee. He didn't like the two of them being friends in the least and set to teach Ron a lesson for befriending white people.

The Sergeant was the worst kind of asshole. He messed with everybody's head. One day the unit went on the trucks to do a fire mission. They drove to the set up range where the artillery was to be stationed. Before the artillery can come, the perimeter must be dug in and reinforced so the weapon can sit on level bails. The Sergeant ordered Danny and Ron to get off the truck and start the sandbag routines. That meant filling up all the sandbags for the complete encampment of that gun. It was no less than four hundred sandbags. Ron and Danny sat all day holding each bag in one hand and a tiny shovel in the other hand with the intention of filling up one sand bag, putting it down then filling up the next one and the one after that.

The rest of the unit had gone off on forest drills in the woods and when they came back the Sergeant was pissed drunk. He smiled as the truck approached the two marines finishing on the second third of the encampment. The next day during the firing drill the Sergeant was drunk again and started to yell at the marines as his jeep approached and he stepped out of the moving vehicle. As he did his wedding band caught on a piece of metal on the door and ripped his finger off. He was bleeding everywhere and artillery exploded all around him as the Sergeant got down on his hands and knees looking for the rest of his finger. The men asked him what he was doing and he screamed at them to find his ring.

"Not the finger sir?"

"If I don't find that ring my wife will kill me."

The next day the Sergeant was drunk and didn't have much to say. The unit saw him the next day and they didn't have much to say to him either. Nobody had much to say to Sergeant Van Guard unless he cornered you somewhere and then he was usually a prick.

One night while Ron was on guard duty he fell asleep and Sergeant Van Guard snuck up behind him and took his rifle. When he woke up, Ron discovered his rifle was gone. Anxiety overwhelmed him and he froze in his post. He felt the cold steel of metal on his temple and looked up to see Sergeant Van Guard staring down the barrel with his finger on the trigger. Ron could not explain himself and prepared his mind for a court martial. Danny made up a story to cover for Ron and they sent Danny to the brig. Danny knew the malicious intent was aimed at both of them and that his friend might not survive the beatings that took place inside that moratorium. After watching Ron heal in the hospital from the hanging and now surrendering himself once more, Danny could only weep for the Virgin Mary and pleaded with the court for responsibility to no avail.

Ron lost his corporal stripes because of the incident. He was busted down from an E4 corporal to an E3 and lost his NCO privileges. Ron began making a plan of retaliation to enact when Danny's sentence expired. It was a Friday night and everyone on base was at the Recreation hall having drinks. Because Sergeant Van Guard was a drunk, he was leading the way. He slurred his speech and spit on the uniforms of the lower ranks desecrating his authority. Because Ron and Danny both lost their NCO privileges they weren't allowed inside the party, so they paid several other marines to keep buying Sergeant Van Guard shots of whiskey. The Sergeant loved whiskey and after more than a bottle full had to be carried to his quarters where after a half hour of sickness on the grass, he managed to crawl into bed.

Ron and Danny had short sheeted his bed with three rattle snakes. Sergeant Van Guard began kicking and screaming and then yelling in terrified shrieks of horror in the darkness, drunk. He was bitten more than fifty times. When Ron left Guantanamo, he gave the Sergeant his medal for good conduct.

Ron had become a guns and artillery specialist and was promoted to the rank of weapons training instructor. He'd been taught to mark points twenty miles away in a 155 Howitzer. The United States military was armed with the most advanced weaponry of the 21st century. The game was to send infantry to find the location of the enemy and mark him out on a grid so the guys on the Howitzers could use even more sophisticated mathematical calculations. This added to the art of war, to see just how dastardly devious and superior they truly could be from long range. It was like shooting ants from outer space with a laser except somebody had to find the anthill. The person setting the coordinates had to be spot on the mark. One half degree off on the dial could mean fifty yards away on the map and an entire platoon would be wiped off the face of the earth.

Chapter 6

**Doris Van Clief accepting the purple
heart on behalf of her son Pete**

Ron arrived in Okinawa in 1963. Okinawa was the home of Karate. Okinawa-te was the ancient Chinese hand form of Karate brought to the chain of islands in the Pacific when different clans warring with mainland China spread out to establish their territories. Those devoted to the martial arts made their way to the chain of islands known as the Ryukyu Kingdom where these arts were mastered. Ron had stepped into a surreal world of his own fantastic imagination. All the comic books and stories he'd ever read as a child came true. The orient was the magical link to the mind, body and soul. His handsome eyes and black skin caught eyes everywhere.

Ron immersed himself in the study of Karate taking up where Masters Duncan and Urban left off. The Chinese spawned the 25 different animal styles of Kung Fu and opened up the chambers of enlightenment. He studied Chinese Karate from an Okinawan master named Shimabuku. Shimabuku was a little old man standing 5'2" who could disintegrate bricks with his punches and kicks. Shimabuku taught the basic

41

weapons of martial arts. Ron learned how to use the sword, sai, tonfa, bo and nunchaku.

He fell in love with the Orient and enlisted for another year on active duty. The Americas were far behind him now, boot camp just a memory and his next assignment stationed him in the Philippines. There he learned Tagalog and studied under Grandmaster Remy Presas, the son of businessman Jose Presas. Remy began studying Arnis with his father, his grandfather Leon Presas, and his uncle at the age of six. By the age of fourteen he had his first stick fighting match with a Sinawali master. Remy knocked the master out with one stick hit. From there Remy traveled across the Philippine Islands learning from the other masters and competing in stick fighting competitions and street fights. By middle age, Presas had mastered the three martial arts of the Filipino descent.

Arnis, Eskrima and Silat the basis of the Filipino weapons based martial arts fighting with sticks, staffs or knives. The three different styles came together pulling out the most efficient techniques which could be demonstrated and taught easily to new warriors going into battle for the first time. The teachings were passed down with Filipino tradition allowing villagers, generally not professional soldiers, a measure of protection against other villages as well as foreign invaders. The style which is now branched under the name Eskrima is rooted in the philosophy of simplicity. Because of this approach, Eskrima and the Filipino martial arts in general are often mistakenly considered to be simple. However this refers only to its systematization, not effectiveness. To the contrary, beyond the basic skills lies a very complex structure and a refined skill set that takes years to master. In a short time Ron was proficient in all three.

In 1964, Ron received orders to be transferred to the Republic of Vietnam. He would finally see some real action. He boarded the LSD Catamount bound for Vietnam. Scuttlebutt was that shit had really hit the fan in Vietnam. The

French had made a mess and the Marines were going in to clean it up before communism spread to the rest of the world. Ron prepared for combat by cleaning all of his gear and his M-16 constantly. No one spoke much. Everyone was apprehensive. Everybody thought they knew what war would be like, but not one of them had ever been fired at in combat. Just yesterday they'd been getting stoned in the whorehouse having a time the 60's hadn't heard about yet. They tried to talk easy but their mouths were dry and the words stuck in the back of their throats.

$200 US per month in 1964 for combat pay went fast on three dollar hookers when every other Tom, Dick and Jerry was getting his cherries blown off in the thick. It was the same ocean that landed GI's on Iwo Jima. The air was tropical and nobody from a mid-western farm knew the difference between Hanoi and Saigon. They left on battleships and aircraft carriers singing valiant songs of glory, chuckling at the lumps in their throats and winding down the butterflies with a hardy-har-har.

When one thousand men landed on the beaches there were one thousand body bags waiting to be loaded. One thousand American flags to drape over the mantle pieces of one thousand American mothers, wives and daughters. One thousand nightmares in a hologram of the worst shit imaginable. Ron feared for his life with the rest of the soldiers. They sweated more from the stress that awaited them than from the heat of the jungle.

"Get these greenies. Not a fuckin' clue. They'll be so smacked up in a week if they ain't dead tonight. They're all fucked. I don't know who signed me up for this shit. I guess it was the thing to do at the time. It beats a job at the fishing canneries. Stinks you know; fish piling in hour after hour, day after day, month after month. Your hair smells like fish. Your fingers and your skin smell like fish. All you eat is fish."

"Sergeant, another shot of this?" asked the corporal passing over a bottle of Southern Comfort.

"That's about it right there, Corporal."

"Doesn't get any better than this, Sir."

"Bite your tongue. What I wouldn't give for a summer night in Alaska right now, out fishing for halibut or hunting a grizzly bear."

"Sir?"

"What?"

"You're wondering."

"So I am. Remember what I told you about thought."

"That it's highly unreliable."

"That's right and now it's time for some slant."

"Yes sir."

"Nothing better than some good pussy to wash down a great whiskey."

"Sir, permission to speak freely?"

"Corporal, permission to go fuck yourself, granted."

"Why do we give a shit about these gooks anyway? They never did nothing to us."

"Smarten up Marine or I'll drag your hippy ass under the wire and hang you on it. Communism's the reason. Remember the Nazis? Whew, this stuff tickles," the Sergeant winced as the sting of oak barrel bits stung his tonsils. "Politics, ya see."

"Ah shit, look at this Bushnigger."

"Son of a bitch, where did he come from?"

"Lord knows we don't need another one of them here."

"Oh well. He's dead already," said the Sergeant checking Ron's sleeves. "He's in the 10th."

The rain poured down with the pressure of sticking your head straight into a full on fire hydrant on a hot day in the city if you were stupid. It rained so hard the drops bounced back up and hit you in the face when you were looking down trying to hide your head. The rain was always there.

They were country boys who were made marines; they were the good old boys; they were the cowboys pulled from the farms; the inner city youth trying to escape the cities of America. The draft started. In order to solve an ever increasing drug problem in America, Government drafted its young men into a war to not only kill them in fighting it, but destroy the minds of the generation which subscribed to it. Hundreds of kilos of heroin were coming back in body bags on every transport. It wasn't hard for the officers to organize the shipment the entire way through. There would never be a court martial because technically it never happened. Everyone was smoking grass. All they did was fuck, shoot up, work out and wait to be called into battle.

Ron ran into Kirk a couple of times. He'd gone into the Air Force. Kirk was running drugs and women. He was partners with some guy in the house of M&Q in town. He was selling heroin to the guys on the base. Other guys were shipping it back in the body bags. The two of them would walk into a store in Saigon stoned out of their minds, armed with M-16s and rob the store owner for everything he had. They could do it because who was going to stop them? The money went straight to opium. They would wake up to a beautiful Asian lady sucking their cocks. Whatever trance they were in, they would go back into and when they'd wake back up there was another jade kimono princess to screw.

They never knew when the call would come. They waited with the generosities of an American culture impressed upon an Asian culture. They had gone from shoeing horses and tilling soil to shooting down the enemy in the line of fire; serving their country and protecting the freedoms and liberties of all mankind. In their minds they were heroes. Nobody ever questioned patriotism. There was only one side in the war. They were marines. There was no time for peace flags and flowers and hippies.

Crowds demonstrated when Ron rolled his tank into Saigon. His fifty ton steel dragon tore apart the road, sending concrete and debris into the heads and faces of all of those people who were too close. The ones that did not move were just run over and left to bleed and die and run over again by the jeeps following behind with the infantry trucks bringing in more soldiers to conquer foreign soil.

It was America's attempt to infiltrate Asia. After the fall of the Nazi party, communism was next on the list to go. The powers that be decided that a weak country like Vietnam and their communist oppressors, the Viet Cong, played a perfect scenario to push the new wave of capitalism on the Asian world. Japan was rebuilding and with another Asian country like Vietnam under the influence of American culture, the scene would be set to take on North Korea once more and finally mainland China, but history would note that the Chinese were an advanced civilization many thousands of years in the making. They were explorers of the new world long before history of the modern world could be documented and re-explored and prophecies can be alluring and haunting.

Ron went into combat as a Military Artillery Occupational Specialist. He was an Artillery 0811 Cannoneer manning a 105mm Howitzer; a canon that fired artillery rounds 12 to 15 miles away on Viet Cong troops with pin drop accuracy. The 105 was a hellraiser weapon. The whole artillery unit consisted of four or five hundred guns shooting at one place. Ron was number one and his team was the number one gun crew in the company.

He manned the panoramic sight. The sights were the eyes and ears of the weapon and were responsible for the tangent and site quadrant, elevation and location and the traversing of the weapon. The quadrant and tangent calibrated the trajectory of the round. The Howitzer fired two foot long shells twenty miles away to the target. When command was given to expend all rounds, he did it fast sending two hundred and fifty rounds consecutively. The Howitzers were all hand loaded. Every shot was like thunder striking the earth. Ron was Zeus. The whole sky lit up purple, green and blue. He listened in a headset to the coordinates over the radio and was so good he didn't have to look at the numbers on the dial to balance the weapon. The guys loading and shooting the 105 were at risk. One would load the barrel and another guy would crank on the firing chain. Lots of guys had their fingers taken off when the mechanism fired.

Ron was eventually transferred to the 155mm self-propelled canon operated by six men. It was a tank-like weapon with a gun built into the front that looked like a prehistoric dinosaur. He was the driver of the gun and had to control the 50 ton vehicle upwards of 50 mph. He lost his hearing in the 105's and the 155's. The fuselage of the tank where the men sat was small. Every sound was magnified. The men were in the firing chamber with the firing pin right in front of them. The difference between the 105 and the 155 was the 155 wasn't single loaded. The shells in the 155 were loaded in a magazine four at a time. A loader would drop them in from the top, Ron would fire the rounds and the loader would put four more in the top. The whole wall of the 155 lined up with HG, high explosives, and other kinds of demolition explosives. The 155 was a walking bomb. The Viet Cong thankfully didn't have tank busters. They were still into rifles and bazookas. But if the 155 took a direct hit from a bazooka the tank would be blown a mile high.

Tanks were not in his destiny. Charlie wasn't into fighting a conventional war. They were dug in deep. Because America was fighting with conventional war tactics in Vietnam, the soldiers found unconventional ways to deal with the stress. Ron was a good marine because he could do his job. But he was still a fuck up. He was a rebel. He would stay out past curfew and come home drunk or stoned. He started doing drugs in Okinawa for recreation and to numb the torture of his hanging. The drugs were the only way to escape the Marine Corps' brainwashing before you were sucked back in again. His mind was never straight after the hanging and he pushed the limits constantly.

He linked up with some friends in the air wing. His next transfer was on a helicopter as a door gunner. He manned the M-60 machine gun. One day, they were on medevac, picking up the wounded and dropping more soldiers into the thick. Charlie opened up with automatic weapons as they flew by. Ron pinned down the enemy attacking the LZ with a blanket of rounds from the M-60. There were wounded in the field. One man lost the lower half of his body. He was gone. Another one got zipped up the spine with an AK-47 as he reached the chopper. Two marines grabbed another wounded man as Ron sat back and mowed the grass until they could get into the air again. After that day he couldn't fly again without the heroin and the war as well as his life, became a horror movie.

His brother Pete was drafted and sent in as infantry. They ran into each other in a whorehouse in Saigon. He was an airborne paratrooper in the 1st cavalry. He looked beat and tired with the soul of a thousand echoes bagged under his eyes.

He was in the real shit. Airborne Rangers were dropped from ten thousand feet with nothing but their kit and the objective: Search and Destroy. There were Punji sticks and tigers; land mines, friendly fire, clay mortars; all the devices men create to destroy men when they cannot create a device to fix men. The problem was that one was never better than the other. It was a stick up from the waist down and it might hurt to see an amputee still playing with the booby traps of war left behind on a footpath in the dense jungle. Ron and Pete shared a few drinks and a couple of whores, contemplating a way out of the madness.

That was the last time he would see Pete alive. Pete had two years to go in the military at that point and then at the age of twenty two, three months in Vietnam, Pete was sent home in a body bag. Ron would take his brother's casket and the pieces of his body that remained home to his mother. Doris was all alone now without her favorite son who was buried in a grave. She could not eat. She could not sleep. Her most favorite thing in the world was gone.

Ron was terrified of the ocean and yet today he swims a mile every morning to Shark Island out his back door down the beach and into the crystal clear waters of the Virgin Islands. When he was five years old his father took him to the beach at Coney Island, carried him out in the water to where he could not see the shore and let him swim back. Allaire Van Clief was a merchant marine who sailed around the world and never fully learned how to swim. He was the bastard child of a Chinook Indian squaw who serviced the pleasures of a deliberate Hasidic mailman. Allaire became a champion boxer raised on the streets of Brooklyn without the luxury of a break. A half eaten apple shared between friends and a garbage can fire to keep warm, were the city's main form of communal welfare that Allaire partook in.

In a tunneling vision for something better, Allaire's face held the eyes of the wolf across the meadows and over the fence somewhere who was watching over his flock. He could smell it on the wind. Then he saw the terror and the frenzy of other merchant marine's ships torpedoed in the crossfire in the middle of a bloody shark attack. There were fifty seven who lost their lives, eaten by the beasts of the deep while the boats sunk and burned all around him. The men screamed and Allaire watched their faces until the breath escaped them and their bloody shrieks fell pale blue, sinking into the depths. There was nothing anybody could have done, but Allaire blamed himself the rest of his life.

Allaire smacked his son across the face. Ron relived the moment like it was yesterday.

"I told you to stay out of the military," Allaire said when Ron came back from Guantanamo before going to Okinawa.

"I'm a marine."

"You think you're a man?" Allaire reared back and socked Ron between the eyes. When Ron woke up again his father was gone.

The marines were there to kill. There were no protests among them and they never thought about it. A protest never solved anything. The marines rolled through Saigon in the 155 self propelled and ran people over who were protesting. The men had been built as marines. There were no hippies. There were no pacifists in the fox hole or in the town. The military builds marines to go into town and take out their Zippo and burn everything down leaving no survivors. Hit it with artillery. There were 'x' amount of rounds they needed to get rid of every month because the defense department was under contract with the arms manufacturers. Before the manufacturers could get paid, the military needed to expend all rounds to keep up with the supply of ammunition.

Modern warfare had become commercialized. The Marine Corp Ron went into had the M1 and then went to the M14, the M15 and the M16 all within two years. Between the 14, 15 and 16, the modifications they made were so sloppy it was obvious they could have done it right the first time. Instead they ripped off the government for millions and millions of dollars because they had a stockpile of M14's, 15's and 16's. Ron would drop down on the deck and the magazines wouldn't work. They were still experimental. It didn't take a captain to realize there was some bad shit happening. The rifles clogged up with mud and started to rust in the swamp. The government was experimenting with the soldiers by having them use the arms manufacturers' weapons and these manufacturers made money selling their weapons to different companies and getting the kickbacks. That was what started Vietnam. It wasn't communism. Anybody on the ground could see that communism wasn't going to come from Vietnam over to America and the marines just wanted to get the fuck out.

It was the government's military complex. Ron took lives for nothing so that some guys could make money on the back end with the armaments and Pepsi Cola, candy or whatever they brought there to make billions of dollars. Vietnam was a big ploy to make money. America wasted 58 thousand lives. That's how many were killed. America left another 60 thousand walking wounded. Everyone who survived wounded or not, had Post Traumatic Stress Disorder.

There is only one way of retaking the torture inside one's mind which is the reenactment of an equal torture upon others. When one is right, the other is wrong and order justifies the cause over any logical field assessment. When you're a 'swamp nigger' in hell there ain't much less than you and you have to pull the trigger on a thousand beady eyes in the white of the moonlight.

The story has been told a thousand times and serves a purpose to burn the retina on a 35mm tracer flashback dropping in and out as we slip and slide between the twelve dimensions; the ethereal film of a shadow on our skin transformed into zombies aiming M16's.

The rain pissed down upon them. When it stopped, the mud caked at their ankles and rashes blistered between their thighs as the GI's marched on. The ground game was too much terror for his mind to handle after he lost Pete who was playing marine ranger, jumping out of planes to clean up the messes made on the ground from miles away by the Howitzers and fighter pilots bombs.

"Flying high got a bird in the sky."

"Copy that leader."

Ron was strapped into his chair around by his waist and his shoulders. The helicopter could go 90 degrees vertical in the air and make an oval back towards earth. Ron would be there like a ride at the carnival with nothing to hold onto but the trigger of an M60 side door gunner.

"Ready to crop dust these dogs," Ron said into the headset, his eyes juiced to the point of bulging from their sockets.

"Standard procedure," the pilot of the UH-1 Huey said dropping down to 150 yards above the deck and the helicopters swarmed into another grass and stick village in the heart of the jungle.

"All routine...Let's tag 'em and bag 'em."

There was nothing to it but to clean up a little mess the boys on the ground made and burn it to the ground with some more napalm. Ron's eyes burned the fire orange of tiger stripes stalking on the trail. He'd been hit up with more than the usual poke of heroin on this hop. It was already a suicide mission. Every mission was a suicide mission. The main objective wasn't bringing soldiers home. There were more where they came from sitting in the parks in San Francisco fucking each other like animals spaced out of their minds. The main objective was to locate Charlie, call in the spot to the Howitzers, lay the smack down and split. If Marines got bogged down, then they had to hold tight and maybe enough people would be killed so the rest could walk away when there were no more bullets.

Ron started trimming up the tops of the trees with a couple hundred rounds from 7.62mm 'Pig' as the birds came in low on the village to wake up any snipers or anti-aircraft threats. The village was alive. There were no women and children. It was a trap and the men remained, eyeing them tauntingly.

Gunfire exploded into the air around the helicopter breaking out the glass in the windscreen and busting the head of the pilot. The tail was hit and the helicopter spun out of control around and around so slowly in the span of all those final flashing moments a marine escapes from to buy and then put away and carry in a pocket. Smoke billowed from the mouth as the blades wound like a pinwheel shining folds of air and cutting down the few remaining seconds of life until the crash.

The Huey pilot was dead. The co-pilot's neck was broken. Ron's sternum was fractured. Hot pieces of shrapnel were still burning into his skin and he could not move. He coughed up blood because his ribs were broken. The splinters tore the soft pink tissue and he sneezed out the bubbly froth from his nostrils. Marines on the field grabbed him and sheltered him. He was bleeding out. A private from the third pulled up his shirt and they put a needle in his vein for the transfusion. He sat in the grass watching the terror all around him and finally as the F-18's crackled over laying a blanket of napalm in the forest. The war was over for him. Ron was going home.

After six weeks in a body cast he had recovered enough to start walking. He couldn't get far enough away from Vietnam and thus began the real nightmare because no matter where he went after the crimes he committed, no matter how he felt about himself, he could not let go of what had made him who he was. He was a killer.

He went to the foot of his bed and opened the lock. He put everything on the bed along with his clothes and other personals. His M-16 rested against the wall. He took the weapon and disassembled it down to its smallest components and then he packed all of his belongings together in his seabag walked out the door and never looked back.

Chapter 7

**Ron's graduation photo
from Parris Island**

He woke in complete darkness, trapped with the smell of dank metal, urine and vileness. The walls shook from the engine room on the upper floors of the ship. His head rocked back and forth on the cold metal ground as the waves rolled under him dragging Ron Van Clief back into hell. The war kept on going.

"Don't panic," he told himself. "At least you're alive. I don't know where that is or for how long it will be, but it is right now that we are breathing."

"Giddy up you fuckin' porch monkey. What's the matter? Shit yourself you filthy baboon?"

The anger channeled so deeply in his mind and he believed what the white people said. They rode him into the ground day and night. He was a marine and he'd been killed by his own kind. He'd saved their lives and they still couldn't care about him. Skin color separated the kind of people they really were.

"They's goddamn coons. And we like our coons in trees. We's gonna hang us a *nigger* tonight and we's gonna hang us another *nigger* tomorrow night until we done hanged all the *niggers* every night for the rest of our lives." The hatred swelled from vehement lumps in their throats. They spit it out so freely. Their voices played over and over in his mind absently as if he remembered them as a story and not the catastrophe which unfolded on him.

"I hope you ain't afraid of the dark!" said the last voice he heard as he was thrown into the room and the steel door slammed shut behind him. "Don't let the Boogeyman get you." There was only a second of light for him to assess his surroundings before he was locked in. The walls were covered in feces. Old dirty blankets soiled the ground and stains of dried urine stuck in puddles on the floor. The light disturbed the rats as they scattered from the blinding yellow bulb into the outside tunnels of maze work in the lower decks.

The images flashed through his mind in the darkness recalling the last days before his innocence had been taken. He'd given up his freedom by signing that paper; freedom of which he never could have known. He was somebody else's property now and they would do with him what they saw fit. They owned him. They made him sleep, breathe and shit when they wanted him to. They sent him on the kinds of missions into the jungle when nobody came back. They'd taken his soul. He pushed away the horrors coming to him and clung to the dearest thing his mind could grab.

His chest was broken; his breath heavy under the confinement of the dark cell in the bottom of the ship. He gasped for air that would not come down from the upper levels. He stood in the darkness trying not to move. He found one of the blankets on the floor and swept the ground using his feet and the blanket as a broom to clear out some space from the dimensions he remembered when the light had shined briefly before.

"What the hell have I got myself into now?" he sighed. "Do they think they can cage me like an animal? Well they have and I don't know how long it will be because the voyage has just started and I don't think they'll pay too much mind about a black piece of shit like me. They're upstairs laughing and playing cards, talking about pussy. Those racist fucks. What the hell did I ever do to them?" He began to cry because he did not understand the hatred. He could not understand the evil or where it came from; that men could be so cruel to one of their own. "I've saved all of their lives and they do not know it. They do not think about it when the bullets are whizzing by and they're screaming for their mothers and I pull them off to safety. They didn't seem to mind that I was a *nigger* then." Then he stopped crying. There was a snap of metal and a small flicker of light as a little door opened. A loaf of bread wrapped in wax paper appeared and then a pitcher filled with water. The door snapped shut again bringing home that same darkness that commiserated papillion.

There was a fury surrounding his feet as the rodent's nostrils were filled with the smell of the bread filling the air. By the time Ron had stepped down to pick up the food, the rats had mobbed it ripping at the wax paper with their teeth tearing it open for the morsels inside. Instinctively he seized the bread, shaking the rats from his dinner as they clung to his hands biting at his fingers. They would not surrender and as long as they could smell the bread they came for him. They climbed up his pants sniffing their way closer to his mouth that could not chew fast enough to release them of their pursuit. He ate the bread though it tasted terrible. He knew he had to because that's all there was to eat. He chewed through the loaf of starchy cardboard choking it down between bites, chewing the way he'd been taught in boot camp grinding it twenty times before he swallowed. He set his mind into a rhythm while he ate to block out the squeals and the screeching from the tide of rodents swarming him. He was close to the border that separated anxiety and serenity when the rats tipped over the steel pitcher spilling out his beverage onto the floor.

Infinity spanned time in each second of the darkness and then a door of light opened up. He put the metal pitcher of shit and piss through the hole and it was replaced with a clean metal pitcher of water and a new loaf of bread in wax paper. The door slammed shut. He stared at the glowing tracer as the darkness faded again. The flash had given just enough light to bring his mind back to the situation he was in.

The torrential panic of suffocation waned against the heat and agony of each fainting breath. He felt the weakness of nausea twist in his stomach and he let it go, masking over it again now with the soothing rhythm and steady tempo of the waves breaking beneath the hull and the engines of the floating hospital taking over 5000 soldiers into the heart of the madness. Loading up the ship with the dead to be brought back and buried and leaving the wounded to be crucified upon the altar of a psychedelic opera.

Ron stared into the darkness of solitary confinement deep beneath the ocean. His mind plunged into a thousand nightmares that came to tear apart the cradle of an infant's innocence. He recalled his first days of boot camp when the guys talked the toughest trash on the way, but then these same guys were calling for their mommies because some guys from Tennessee whooped their asses and took their toothbrushes. He had not buckled under the pressure of crying and screaming, he choked back the tears while the Marine Corp tore him apart and rebuilt him. Man's ignorance had cast him as a slave. Man's follies had designed a way of life intentionally destined to fail, based on principles oblivious to any golden rules. Without punishment against crimes of bigotry and hate that society births and condones through the tolerance of evil; inherently good natured people believe what they are told and carry those words as truth. Ron joined the proudest of all services to transcend the stereotype of hatred, to become something greater for the better of mankind. Even though everybody's smile was broken and they all had the same tattoos, nothing could change the fact that he was black.

"We're going to hang you, *Nigger*," was what they said as they mobbed him in a laughing torrent of beatings.

He was to spend 30 days in solitary confinement on the trip to San Diego. Had it been five days already? Had it been seven? He couldn't remember. His only contact to the outside world was that little flash of hope opening quickly then snapping shut again, refreshing him with the warm pitcher of water and bread in wax paper. He dreamed of the smell of asphalt in the Bronx. The past flashed in his mind irrelevant of time; still so significant. He needed them now. He needed Kirk and Pete. He started to wonder of the fool he'd become to let them treat him this way. These pigs had made him lower than dirt. They spit on him. They shit on him while he slept. They pissed on his face and because he defended himself as a marine knows how to, they punished him, imprisoning him in the darkness ready to be pulled out when they needed a gimp to play with. The rage swelled inside him and he took another deep breath exhaling his present solitude replacing it with a happier time.

In the dark and the dampness, the rats covered his body. The few times he slept, he was awakened by the nibbling in his ears from the lice that were festering on his scalp, drawing bedsores to his skin. He scratched at his eyes as if feigning from an intravenous opiate transfusion. He didn't know if he could go one more day without packing it in; beating his brains against the metal wall, splattering them into a thousand pieces of his own imagination. The past was too much and he was in way too deep. There was nowhere to go in the darkness. He bit on his thumbs until they bled. But what kind of a man was he if he didn't prevail? Even perseverance in the ultimate face of adversity was too much for a country or a cause. And he was just another black man.

"Help me!" he screamed.

He saw dead people as his mind struggled to make sense of what was going on. One thousand faces exploded at the mushroom of a .50 caliber round. Bits of blood flew everywhere in the midst of a chopping helicopter blade.

"I see your Kung Fu is strong," He stuttered in the darkness. He spoke to himself in a voiceover of kung fu movies he'd seen.

"Yes, you are a worthy opponent," he switched characters.

"Maybe you will become a smart man and leave this world behind. Find riches you will, hmm. Make your bastard parents happy. Then again maybe you won't."

"There can be only one."

"So, you think you have what it takes to beat me?"

"I welcome the challenge my friend."

He spoke to himself in the darkness until he'd played the entire movie in his head; the fight scenes and the music that played when the villain entered on camera. The charades bought him some time, but when the movie was over, the banging from the boiler room reminded him of his situation and what he must do to survive. Right now that meant shivering against the heat and shortness of breath. How long had it been?

Chapter 8

Ron wanted to be home in New York but he did not realize that drugs and filth had taken over the city. He remembered the time when he and his brother Pete came home to find Allaire unconscious leaning against the hot radiator. His shoulder and upper arm were stuck to the radiator. The smell of bacon filled the air while the iron heater cooked his burning flesh. Pete and Ron pulled him off the radiator, peeling his skin from his neck and back. They both cried and screamed out for somebody to come and help them as their father bled there on the floor with drool pouring from the side of his mouth. Allaire was so smacked out on heroin he didn't even moan. He didn't move. His eyes were lost inside the back of his head and his arm was kinked up in a muscle spasm as though he'd been frozen in a prison camp on the way to watching his friends burn in an oven. Ron hated the memories of his father. He beat his fists against the walls of the darkness, kicking and punching the metal box, bending it out to break it at the seams of its weld.

"Why? I only wanted to impress you," he cried at last. "I only wanted to make you proud of me. I wanted to become something you would admire." His own arms and neck seized up on him as he made the face his father had made while burning on the floor. He choked the tears that ran down the back of his throat like the open flood gates on Mt. Olympus. "Make me a God." He shot bolts of lightning through the darkness at Zeus provoking a flat stone eyed gaze in his direction. Ron took the serpent from the sea and threw it at the moon with Herculean strength causing the giant man in the clouds to scratch his head and yawn at the curious black figure who was causing such a stir.

Everywhere he went he was a *nigger*, he heard. No coloreds allowed. He wanted to be free from this prison beneath the ship but that was just a dream he held onto. He counted in his mind trying to calculate what day it was. When he was put into solitary there were 10 days left to the 4th of July.

He felt nostalgic for Brooklyn in the summer. The smells of the old Italian stores filled his lungs and he wiped the sweat from the back of his neck with a handkerchief that he dipped in an open fire hydrant flooding the street where neighborhood school kids were playing on a hot summer afternoon in the city with firecrackers popping all around. He could taste the mustard and the juice as he bit down into a hotdog from the vendor on the street corner.

And then the only fireworks he could see were the flashes of blazing fury from the muzzle of the .50 cal machine gun, strapped in the helicopter. The world he saw was a cartoon as they swooped down low over villages where there might be Viet Cong. He'd been in the middle of a war and he didn't know how many lives he'd taken. The darkness filled his mind until his eyes projected the same trauma over and over. Brooklyn was gone. Though he'd seen it just last week he could not become familiar with it. There was no comfort anymore. The brief world he'd lived in since boot camp had shuttered him off from civilian mentality. He was made to kill. They'd taken everything from him; even his memories. He could not find them now. He could only find the will to hang on for one more day to get his brother's coffin home. He flashbacked to the jungle.

"We have a baker's dozen," said the blackhawk pilot on his headset, eyeing the rice paddies and the first few huts. 'Let's give 'em the shake down."

"Copy that."

Ron lifted the safety catch from the grip of the machine gun while lining his eye down the sites of the barrel. Like stacked cards in a folly of wind, without direction or purpose, just flittering through the air, they fell one by one. Asian children screamed and women grabbed them and ran from their huts to hide in the jungle but it did not matter. They folded in half where the bullets the size of a man's thumb ripped through them leaving the last moments of their life peering back up at death from above. The man in his young years of adolescence was trained for only one motivation, one destiny, and one objective; seek and destroy. Kill or be killed. Just kill.

"He really mows 'em down, don't he," said the pilot through the headset to the pilot in the other helicopter.

"I'm the best there ever was," Ron screamed though there were no words in his voice. The heroin in his veins was blasting his heart out in beats per second. His eyes aligned with the tracks of coursing rivers of opiate in the hottest depths of hell. The repeated fire in his eardrums screamed out for all sins of eternity to be reconciled. He needed the drug. He had to have it in his blood. Without it he started to shake and shiver. And there was no room for air in this tiny prison cell. The man he punched deserved it for what he had done.

"I may be a *nigger*, but I'm still a human and no man is going to take a shit on me."

His clothes still smelled from the other man's defilement and now from the smeared excrement molding in the box they put him in. His neck clenched up until his teeth threatened to shatter and he was sure he would swallow his own tongue. And now there would never be closure. He'd hit a civilian on the ship who went to the bathroom on him while he was sleeping. When he woke, a group of GI's sat around him laughing. They didn't try to hide who did it. The civilian was proud of what he'd done and the rest of the GI's sang him praises. They didn't want *niggers* in their country. They didn't want *niggers* in their army either.

The darkness was several days now and he had eaten only bread and water. The heat was draining him as his body sweat out every sip of water he put down. His belly was bleating and his mind began to travel but without the drug he was trapped and he could not escape his own itching body crawling with ants gnawing at his brain.

The pinning from the engine room rattled the walls and the floor around him and his body hummed consistently, melting his flesh against his hot metal bed. The beads of sweat around his forehead turned into a waterfall down his face and his shirt and pants were soaked and the water they gave him through the little door of light was not enough to fill him up from what he was losing in dehydration.

He was dying now and all of his years of combat training in the jungle, in the Carolinas, and in the backstreets of New York could not save him. These tools were lost to him. He knew he would die now but then realized he would not be so lucky. He would have to endure.

"I know that the bread is not enough. The water is not enough. I should not speak to myself aloud because there is no more air left for that. They know they will suffocate me and when I die I will just be a *nigger* they got rid of. At least I'll be a *'dead nigger'*."

And then the other side of his brain spoke. He'd been through hell already but at least inside the box he wasn't getting shot at. As bad as it smelled he didn't have to be with those prigs. Then again, living with a white man was better than sleeping in other men's shit and piss. Or was it? It did not matter now which was better because it didn't change the situation. He tried to plead with his situation hoping there were worse things a man could go through. He'd already been hanged. He'd been beaten to a bloody pulp. He'd survived boot camp and the first six months of Vietnam. At the end of the list, the worst possibilities outweighed the bad ones. His mind was useless. He had to rely on his body to save him.

Again the nightmare took him back to the hospital bed in North Carolina. His face wrapped in gauze and his broken chest bandaged. He knew it wasn't long now before they would pull the plug or just give him something lethal to put him out. Ron gritted his teeth chomping at the sweat from the hot dark box.

"It will piss them off more if I live. Everybody likes to see us *niggers* hanging from trees in the orchard, swinging in the afternoon sun and a cold glass of lemonade to wash down the view from the porch. It would only burden them further by making them carry me out dead and unsporting. Play the animal."

Ron had never been racist. He'd never retaliated against the hateful remarks of bigotry directed at his skin color. He let the words ricochet off until they became fists which beat him and his only will was to survive. Ron thought of the sex den in Saigon and lost his mind in some wet mess. He sweat into the scabs around his wounds through the stitches in his face, hands, feet and ribcage. He would kill for a hit of opium and some sweet creamy slant.

They'd all been with prostitutes in Vietnam and Ron fantasized about them now as he put a face in his mind and played out the pornography in the darkness. The stench from the decaying box subsided and the drumming from the engine left. He escaped into the countryside and for a minute could smell the scent of spring blossoms from the cherry trees floating on the breeze on a fresh afternoon in the Southeastern United States. Drilling it stoned into the warm, wet and beyond, like an infinite cave that discovered it had an ending and then back to the beginning again.

He tasted that sweet sweat on his tongue. He licked those tiny nipples like a child laps at ice cream dripping on the sidewalk in sticky puddles. They rubbed their fingers through his short faded hair and he escaped the darkness. But it was miles since defloration and the leagues of Asian whores he piled under his pillow were no better than the brown sugar to spike an arm with. He was still in debt to the pimps in Saigon and Okinawa and it didn't matter if he was going back to New York, the Papisan would come to collect. Without that spike now, he was lost. In the darkness there was a voice. It was the gentle whisper of the master Peter Urban.

"Focus breathing," he said. "Use the opponent's strengths against him. If he starts to pull, go with him and pluck his eyes out."

Pulled back into his prison once again from the dream, Ron broke free from the virtual journey and began to meditate and center himself in the tiny metal box cooling it down; breaking its walls apart; opening it up to a boundless space; creating the Nissei Goju technique.

The cell at the bottom of the ship was an oven in the darkness. The heat sucked away all air and burned up all moisture. Ron could not tell if his eyes were open or closed. His broken chest puffed in spasms and when he swallowed he choked. The daily ration of bread was barely keeping him alive. When he was able to lift his arms, the tin of water cracked his lips and he would fall from the surge of the cool water hitting his overworked body. Ron stepped into his fall and pulled the delirium from his mind. He put panic and anxiety at arm's length and began to breathe slowly; choking on the deep inhales in his stomach and coughing up the sheath of straw pitched into his lungs.

In the darkness he put his hands up to the shadows and pushed them away. He grabbed them by the throat and swept them to the ground. Over hand crosses, jabs, elbows, knees and roundhouse kicks. In the space of six feet, in the darkness he practiced routines. Every time was perfect. Every breath he inhaled strengthened his will to stay alive. The odds overwhelmed his sanity and when he felt the shadows once again, he could not hold the tears back any longer and he cried like a child, but there was nobody there to comfort him.

The engine room rumbled the long journey back from Saigon. The tapping from the giant pistons swinging down the hammers split open his mind. They'd taken full control and tore the rest of his mind apart. Voices called out from everywhere inside his brain. He could feel his skull crack open as they peered inside his head with their microscopes and their tape recorders and their theories and their medicine. He needed it now and he could not kick out at the shadows because there was nothing to hold. Ron was hollow and the tunnel was calling his soul as his body clenched up and screwed its way through the back of his spine and out through his teeth. In the darkness he had nothing to stop his locking jaw and so he bit his finger until he could rip a strip of linen from his trousers before his teeth turned into fine sand from all the grinding. He choked on the blood from his knuckle and gagged as he swallowed the cloth, retched with feces and filth. He collapsed in a seizure until his head beat the voices out against the floor.

He could see his mother Doris crying. She sat in front of the window in the kitchen of the small railroad flat car watching the snow fall in Brooklyn. The snow whited out the sky; gathering on the street lights and parked cars and on the shoulders of people strolling in the streets on Christmas Eve. She mourned Peter. She blamed God for taking him away from her and she hated the world around her and would never forgive herself.

He felt her love in the bottom of that hollow pit. She had seen the ghosts in his eyes when he buried Allaire. There was so much hate and resentment and she could see the man her son had become; cold and murderous on the edge of a lost place somewhere she had never seen. And when she heard the sound in his voice when he called her from the jungle telling her Peter had been killed in action, she accepted that he had abandoned hope and that he was only waiting to die. But somehow Ron was brought back to life again and tortured in front of her over and over like a clockwork's movement ticking the seconds of sanity away from her Christian faith.

Doris instilled faith in them when they children. She believed in tough love. The Van Clief family was never a happy family but it was a disciplined family. Allaire kept the painful memories of sinking ships and burning bodies floating at sea on the surface for everybody to see. He would go into a trance in the middle of supper or while watching the clouds in the sky and he would tear up. There was nothing to stop his emotions from pouring out except the spite he felt for the world which had made him this way. Instead of crying, his tears turned to rage unleashed on the nearest child within his reach. Doris tried to comfort him, holding his head on endless nights until the sun came up and by then, even she had tired of his demonic curse. The two had been married long before the war, gone through the depression and eaten what mere rations rats could not touch. They wore patches that holes could not clothe. His only release was the boxing ring and he destroyed himself and others in it.

When Allaire came back from World War II after being torpedoed the third time, there was a piece of him that did not come home. That part of him was lost forever at sea with all the drowned men floating in that swelling beast of God's wayside.

Ron caught a breeze blowing through the dense humidity of the jungle to his hole in the ship. Everywhere was one place and no place at one time. He was lost in the world overlying with the obscenity of vagrancy, disheveled and preoccupied, pulling his mind in and out of a mental flashback where sanity was abandoned for the natural instinct to survive.

"Say, this stuff is all right."

"Man did you ever get over to that one place on the back street between village and the temple?"

"Yah, they got some badass little honeys."

"Pulled this stuff in from Rangoon. Smokes good. Gets you really out there, you know what I mean?"

"Yah, I know what you mean."

One of the cracker officers from somewhere in the hate mongering south was torching some marijuana in the chamber of his machine gun. Another soldier sucked slowly through the barrel of the gun inhaling the smoke into his lungs then sat back with a haze in his mind.

"Make sure you pulled the primer."

"Yah, got it. I think."

"How many stars you think there are?"

"Sure are a lot of them. I bet more than a billion."

"There's way more than that. There's more than anybody can count. One day we'll walk on the moon."

"Probably."

"I want to go to the moon."

"The only place you're going O'Hara is the mental hospital if you make it out of this fuckin' shit."

"Kennedy wanted to go to the moon but he got his ass shot."

"Thank God for the asshole in charge now or we'd be missing the war."

"Hey, that's the President you're talking about."

"Yah, whatever. He's got us over here fighting gooks. I want to go to the moon."

"It ain't so bad here," O'Hara said lying back exhaling the smoke.

"This is the worst kind of shit. Tigers bite your face off when you're sleeping. Step out of line and blow your dick and your balls all over the guys around you. This place would make a nice getaway vacation spot if it weren't so Goddamn chock full of Charlie on the ground coming out of every little fuckin' shadow."

"It ain't that bad.'"

"Fuckin' hell it's not. Get me the hell out of this jungle and I'll be happy to sit on mama's front porch for the rest of my life and not say shit to nobody. Let me blow my leg off and collect a pension from the government. At least I'll get off better than most. I don't give a damn about no slant eye. What do you think, Shit Bird?"

"What do I think about what?" Ron asked.

"This is some good shit."

"You reckon a *nigger*'s worth as much as one of these zipper headed sons of bitches? We should trade all the *niggers* in America for the pussy over here."

"You think that's a fair trade?"

"Who gives a fuck? I know it's not a fair trade but who says life's fair? Show me one place in the constitution where the word fair is written."

"Smoke *Nigger.*"

"Take a fuckin' hit. If you're going to die anyway you might as well be stoned out of your fucking mind. You *niggers* are always smoking this shit back home anyway. Where did you say you were from? Baton Rouge?"

"Brooklyn, Mother Fucker."

The reality was that in some groups the officers were so messed up and racist that after the platoon had gone in and dusted off everything in its path, they would hunt down whatever African was amongst them. They needed all the guns they could get for the cleanup but after that it was time to hunt; preferably somebody who'd been trained to hunt and kill; for better competition. He was always looking over his shoulder for one of his own guys to cut his throat. He snuggled his M-16 closer to his chest.

"Now, don't get ahead of me on this one."

"You's an educated Negro, is ya not? Got yourself put in some shit where you can hit a fuckin' pissant on the dick from fifty miles away. One man in a company can do that and that saves lives. Every little dick you blow up gets us more ground and kills more of them."

"I guess so."

"They're wasting good American lives out here in the jungle and keeping some *nigger* safe 20 miles away. Seems to me this war's gone backwards."

"I'm here, ain't I, you cracker headed son of a bitch?"

"Let's not get hostile.'"

"It was backwards before I was a black man who came along to help keep your punk ass alive. You punk Mother Fucker. Give me that."

"Steady, my Black Corporal."

"Don't blow your fucking head off now. That's it. Take a little weight off your mind. Don't be bothered by the subtle differences between us, we're engaging in logic and the reason why you're still alive. They didn't give us a stupid Negro to protect us good ole boys? Nah, they put us with a lucky one."

"Henry you're so high you don't make sense."

"I follow you."

"He's talking about politics."

"That's right my clever little fellow."

"My point is that they got us out here killin' everything that fuckin' moves right? Hell, I don't know if the next girl who's gonna suck me off will pull a hand grenade on us when I'm ready to put it in her throat. So, if we's gonna be killin' gooks, why don't we just kill the men? Their women are worth something. Hong Fang Lee can suck a dick through a cocktail straw. You should see her."

"That's a small straw."

"Maybe with your dick it's possible."

"It don't matter. Balls and all. And that's my point, Corporal. We killin' all the things that might work for us. We could start our own little society away from society. Right here in this jungle. And do you know what that means?"

"That you're the mayor?"

"For one, but on the other that makes you the only *nigger,* so I guess if there's some kind of use for ya, you might be worth a piece more than a gook whore."

"Hey that's enough," said the Sergeant.

"Don't you worry. We're just playin' around. Speaking philosophically and all. It's cool baby. Take your Negro and go pet his fuckin' head or whatever it is you do with one of them. I'm going to get me a stuffed *nigger* anyway for my dogs to play with in the yard."

Ron did not say a word, but sprung with the blade of his K-bar knife against the soldier's windpipe.

"Don't be so sensitive."

"Henry," he said finally, "they might let me live long enough to feed your penis to you. And when you're lying there with your stomach blown up all around the forest crying to your mother, I'll walk over to the tree for you where the last

73

piece of your dick will be hanging and in your last breaths when what you should say is sorry for being an ignorant piece of white trash, but you'll ask me to give a letter to your mommy and trying to get one last smoke from me. Instead of doing that, I'll reach down, right between the tears dripping down your pale face as your eyes roll back and the last thing you experience will be when I stick your cock in your mouth and choke you out on it. How does that sound?"

"Ain't no *nigger* going to talk to me like that."

"Well then you're going to have to do something about it."

The Sergeant raised his gun to Henry's temple.

"Sit down," he said.

"Why don't we just smoke some more of this shit and look at the stars and try not to get killed tonight by whatever the fuck is out here?"

"It's rather peaceful when you just sit back and listen to the crickets and the frogs and the birds; speaking in the night."

"Happiness is overwhelming me."

"Time to strap on. This shit's better than candy."

"Sugar in my coffee."

"Keeps everything alive."

"Runs through the veins and makes you bullet proof, my man."

"There's nothing like flying with God."

"And you think there's a God?"

"Right here, man," Cowboy said holding up the bag of heroin.

"Who wants to feel anything when your legs are blown off anyway?"

"That's the spirit."

"Knock that shit off."

"Take it easy, Cowboy. You'll get yours. There's enough of this shit for the whole draft."

"They're going to need it with as many ghosts that are running around this place."

"You didn't get this stuff from Rangoon did you?"

"No, this is straight out of Cambodia. One hundred percent pure heroin. Hot doggy. And we even got enough needles for the Negro."

Ron had saved all of them many times. They had saved each other. They were the raw grit that rubs against your retinas in the desert without water. The kind of men who do bad things to people who are supposed to have done even worse things and that's how the media spins it so that one side's good guys are beating up the bad guys and it's a race for the news reporter to get out the story first. But one hundred thousand novels written, movies scripted or acts spliced together at the scenes, would never bring one young soldier; regardless of creed or color back to life.

Fox trotter opened up his first aid kit and took out the rubber band and tapped his veins with childish impatience. The spoon clinked against his fingernail and Alpha Company Bravo (or Albert from Cincinnati), covered the glow from the flames in the darkness as the heroin began to bubble. Wrap up the elbow, vein out and go; back it up and find the cherry. Push the plunger and hit the stars forever.

"Delta Alpha Niner. Do you copy?" Came in over the radio and Cowboy turned it off.

"They say this equipment is infallible. I say, that just doesn't work for me."

Ron watched them one by one until it was his turn.

"Don't be afraid," Cowboy said as he flicked the needle with his finger. "I'll give you just the right amount. I won't let you die. You're my little *nigger* baby with your cute little *nigger* toes."

"I've been killed by crazier rats than you, Adolph. You don't have what it takes to kill me.'

"Sure! Why not? But that's enough for now. We're on the same side. Who wouldn't believe us? But that's ridiculous really. Sit back and take your medicine. Does it help if I say I'm sorry?"

Ron did not flinch when the needle pricked his vein, laying down one more mile of track. His fingertips numbed a bit when Cowboy pulled back on the plunger sucking the dark crimson waves into the bowels of the sea then expunged into stormy darkness. He stared into Cowboy's eyes threatening to beat the juice as it mixed in his blood stream. His head got light and then he pulled the ends of the tourniquet loose and the stars became his movie theater; the leaves and branches his bed and the reality of men hunting him in the night, his cartoon dreams.

But he could never sleep again. He could never sleep because even when the platoon was dug in, he could not trust that they would not do him in or shoot him in the head while walking through the swamp, leaving him there to disappear in the decay of the tropics.

It is like a pack of stray dogs gone wild. There are the little dogs which must fight the alpha male and then there are the dogs that run alongside and support the winner; scrapping the spoils of victory. There are no pacts. There are only opportunities. When there are fewer scraps, there are fewer opportunities for some and more opportunities for others. The order of balance is shifted once again until the dominant submission has recessed.

Chapter 9

The Warrior – 1965 through 2002 (900 tournaments)

Mosquitoes were the size of half dollars. The rats were as big as dogs and sounded like cattle stampeding at night. When the marines were in the field, they ate rats every chance they got considering them quite tasty; and when they weren't stuck in the bush they still ate them. Rat burger was a delicacy and the boys were just happy to eat meat. They tasted delicious but one wouldn't want to get bitten as they were infested with fleas and rabies. The soldiers' minds became riddled with the anomalies of Asian culture. The battle fatigue turned them into the ghosts of medieval warriors running around in the shells of American bodies.

There was never an explanation for the torture they inflicted. It was normal at a poker game to use the ears of enemies for ante and a raise. No one thought to question these things because everybody was doing them. Ron was caught in an alternate pre-medieval dimension, disconnected from the rest of his generation. Chuck Berry and Elvis were joined by the Beatles changing the way people looked at music. The sounds came through on the radio. The mind altering substances turned warfare in the jungle into a cartoon. The scene was beyond the writer's imagination. The rules of war were different. The chain of command supported torture and there were minimal repercussions for the atrocities soldiers committed which under typical review would have led to direct court-martials sending the lot of them to the loony bin.

Waterboarding was a prevalent form of interrogation. It was the precursor for modern interrogation tactics. When the marines needed information from a captured enemy, it was not above them to piss and shit on the prisoner if it led to the capture of an enemy target or if it meant saving the lives of other marines. Both sides in the war put their prisoners through the worst hell imaginable. Both sides cut the testicles off their prisoners. Pregnant women were waterboarded. Enemies weren't just tortured to talk, they were tortured to death. People were tortured so bad that when the pain became unbearable they made up stories because they had already told the truth and had nothing left to say. They just wanted the pain to stop. They would give away everything. The soldiers tortured people who knew nothing. On the verge of tears themselves, the only way out for an interrogator was to finish the victim with a bullet in the head. Misery was the closest proximity to humanity.

Vietnam was like the Spanish Inquisition all over again. They smoked grass and shot dope in the hopes that when the high subsided, the war would be over and the marines could walk away and go home. The 60's would prove to be a pivotal time in world history. The Vietnam era became an awakening for the entire world.

Nobody would ever forget the picture of the Vietnam War. The years after played like static in movies the soldiers might have seen when they were children. Years later, they still saw flashes from the same movie. The movie might have been a good movie or a funny movie, but the dreams were the bad dreams; the worst shit they'd ever seen. No matter how many psychotropics and antidepressants they give veterans it will not change the horror they feel for the rest of their lives. It would never change. Ron would wake up shaking for the next forty years.

This was a different game than the streets of Brooklyn. There was a game he and Pete would play; throwing knives on the floor as close to the other person's foot as possible. Ron would always stick the blade right next to Pete's shoe. Pete however, always stuck the blade into Ron's foot. No matter how many times they played the game Ron would never flinch and Pete would stick him every time.

Pete was gone now. He was dead. The truck he was riding in through the jungle ran over a land mine and the explosion blew up right beneath Pete's seat blowing fragments of metal through his torso and mangling his limbs with shards of pain, leaving him to bleed out screaming. It's unfortunate in war when one does not die suddenly in shock, but with agony and time to see life flash before your eyes. Too much time flashes and it doesn't kill one quickly enough. They're in the horrific reality of seeing their guts blown out around them.

Ron had the taste of blood on the back of his teeth. The tiny metal door of light snapped open again. There was nowhere to urinate in the dark four cornered closet so Ron had utilized his water pitcher. The man brought his loaf of bread in wax paper and asked for the pitcher and when he saw that it was full of piss, the man began to curse and then something in his mind stopped him. He pushed a clean pitcher of water through the light and snapped the door shut again.

"Dirty breed," the guard whispered as he walked away.

Ron heard the snap of the door shutting over and over in his head as if it were seconds ago. Tick tock tick tock. He counted to a thousand and then he counted to a million and then the light snapped opened. He had to wipe his ass with the wax paper and he pushed it through in the pitcher now filled with piss. A fresh pitcher came through and another loaf of bread with wax paper. The routine became insanity. It went on for an eternity it seemed and the voices inside his head started to betray him.

At least it was something, he considered. The box didn't offer the comforts of home, but he'd heard of worse. In Russian prisons, solitary confinement was a big hole in the ground thirty feet down. There was no way out and maybe once a day some scraps of food were thrown in. The guards kept you there as long as they wanted then brought you outside without clothes in the freezing cold to walk around corpses and rotten skeletons of the men, women and children who were there before you. Their lifeless grins behind decaying smiles that were missing teeth were a reminder of the hell you were in. You could not hold back the vomit that suffocated the lungs until the belly threw up the bile into the air turning the stomach inside out, eating itself in the void of madness and space of hunger.

Ron screamed. It had been twelve days in the bottom of the ship. His mind scanned the universe and fell upon the master's feet. He did not know how long he had been in the darkness. He told himself stories and tried to remember the good parts of his childhood. But his hatred of the world since Brooklyn drew him from his childhood and it was the ones who'd killed him whom he vowed revenge upon. He would do anything for a pipe of opium at the Papisan's. When the light snapped open again Ron asked the shadow on the other side of the darkness how long it had been. The shadow shifted as if considering whether or not to respond and then without word the dark turned on again. He screamed. He punched the walls with his fists until they bled down his wrists and his hands were broken. He screamed out to God. He screamed out to his father.

"You son of bitch. I hate you. You Mother Fucker. I hate you."

Chapter 10

Ron the Policeman, 1965-1969

Flight of the Dragon was playing at the theater in Brooklyn. It was an hour and a half film. Bruce Lee was the first on the scene in a major motion kung fu film. When the credits were rolling the people started stumbling out and when the trademark flashed, the lights came on. A black man in a long black coat sat hunched over in his seat numbered H-13.

The theatre boy came in to sweep, pick up the trash and the scattered popcorn before the beginning of the next show. He tapped the man on his shoulder and when the man did not stir, the boy shook him gently rolling back the head of Allaire Van Clief. There was a strip of black inner tube on the floor. There was a needle in his arm. There were shrouds of black in his forgotten eyes.

Allaire Van Clief wrapped the band tight and slid the needle into his arm over and over again until the lights of the movie theatre came on and it was time to go. When the lights went out Allaire Van Clief did not get up. He did not move at all.

"You son of a bitch. I loved you and you'll never know it. And because you'll never know it I hate you for it. You called me a coward and I am not a coward. I am tougher than any of those mother fuckers you've ever known. I'm tougher than Kirk and I'm tougher than Pete was and he's dead and you put his death on my hands. I'm tougher than you. I loved you even though you beat me. I could not help you with your nightmares. I am in hell, too," Ron whispered and then he wept.

He slept and he dreamt. He floated high above New York City, flying like he did in his dreams when he was a child. The Statue of Liberty where dreams were made waded in upon the concrete jungle. Up into the clouds, the rain and the sunshine he floated. He slipped below the clouds and dropped in on Okinawa.

"Me love you long time. Me suck you good. Me like soldier boy. Me like you."

He was exotic, black and they swarmed to him like bees to the flowers in the parks in the summertime when all the girls are wearing dresses with their hair pulled back and looking their best. They climbed on him like monkeys on fruit. Black men in the orient were so out of the ordinary, they became legendary before the masses of curious onlookers.

But the dream did not have a happy ending.

"Pay me. Pay me," they pawed.

And then Papisan was grinning over him with those yellow teeth and breath stinking of plum wine. Papisan laughed holding out his hand clenching the heart from Ron's chest squeezing out coins clinking to the ground.

There were a limited number of hookers in Saigon. With 25,000 servicemen and less than a thousand prostitutes, everyone had the clap or gonorrhea. He stood in the penicillin line with his commanding officers as they waited for the moldy tablet to cure their burning Johnsons. He owed money to the Papisan. Every cent the military paid him went to the Papisan who waited outside the gates of the military base for all the GI's to pay up. He couldn't skip out either. Papisan was the Mafia. He'd seen what happened to people who crossed Papisan. One particular case involved a soldier who liked to beat the girls. It wasn't good enough for him that they only cost $3 a piece and did whatever you wanted. Papisan put him in a room with one of the girls who then slipped him a Rufie. Papisan's men took three six inch nails and pounded them into the floor with a hammer. When the soldier woke up in the morning he found himself sitting up bleeding with incredible pain as he discovered three spikes had been driven right through his scrotum.

Another soldier who liked to beat the women was walked to the window of a girl's bedroom. A piano wire was fastened around his genitals and a brick secured on the other end. Papisan threw the brick out the window. The military didn't say a word. Papisan was the law and he was another thing for Ron to look forward to when he got out of this tiny metal box on another death mission out of Saigon.

Ron stirred in his sweating stinking sleep, flying through the air again in the hurricane winds of a monsoon; a rainstorm of bullets piercing his body. When the storm ended the sky was still cloudy. The grass was wet and the rain left the tombstones with shades of gray where his father rested in peace. Ron knelt on the freshly plodded grass amongst the wreaths and bouquets of flowers.

"I don't know how to forgive you," Ron whispered, "I cannot blame you for what you have done. You did what you had to do and that is all I am trying to do now."

Ron grabbed his own forearm and scratched at the burning boils bubbling under the leathered scar tissue. It was too much. Sometimes it is. Sometimes one forgets to brush their teeth. Ron woke again in that swelling pit in the bottom of the ship screeching that twang of cymbals in hateful song.

500 pushups; two thousand sit ups…his mind wandered. He was alone in his room in the small railroad flat on the East side during the winter. On a blank sheet of paper he drew out in detail the character of Donald Duck. He drew Mickey Mouse and Woody the Woodpecker. He drew all the Disney characters, the comic book characters and the cartoons from Warner Brothers; Popeye, Superman and Green Lantern.

He played arithmetic and science. He painted Van Gogh, Picasso and Guaghan in his mind surrendering to schizophrenia. All he'd ever wanted to do was paint and they'd painted him black.

He wanted to paint a sign for the world. He wanted to take their guns away, paint their faces with smiles and he couldn't. He was being taken back to hell to kill the faces he did not know. In his mind he relived the scenes of war. The thick of the heat came down low zipping through every fourth guy in the platoon leaving them screaming in pieces. He filleted the sternum of a Viet Cong soldier with his bayonet through the heart and rubbed the warm release that was sticky between his fingers, feeling the spirit of Native America long before the disease and delirium of small pox crippled their will. The image of the soldier's face changed and Ron held his father in his arms again as he died with the overdose of heroin saturating his life. He liked to think that his father told him then that he loved him and that they made their peace with each other. He was going back into hell and they would meet again there.

The days and the rations of bread in wax paper and pitchers of water for him to drink and then piss in as well as using the wax paper to sit on surmounted upon insanity. He knew he was living in the piss and shit of other men who had been tortured like this before him. Did any get out alive?

Insomnia befell him. When there is no light there can be no day. There can be no hours but minutes of infinity piling up and weighing the mind down. Time is spent counting the seconds in your head trying to remember what number you left off with, stripped of the companionship of a master timepiece. There are no leaves blowing in the wind, no feeling of the morning waking with a sunrise. No sunshine burning in the red haze of an afternoon sunset. There was only the darkness counting the seconds to reprogram.

He only had six months left and he was out. They'd already hanged him and they couldn't kill him. He'd tried to find the bastards who did it. He wrote a letter pleading with Senator Kennedy to look into the matter further but that put him in more trouble. The Senator wouldn't let a snappy little 'colored kid' bring down the entire Marine Corp. They would keep him quiet in the jungles somewhere in Southeast Asia and he'd probably be dead within a week because 1 out of 3 were dead already.

They sent him to hell thinking they could kill him but they couldn't. They'd made him the ultimate assassin and he was disposable. Losing a white man messed with your Johnnies at the end of the day. Losing a black man was like getting a flat tire on your way to work. A pain in the ass because it costs you time and money but a manageable accident not to lose too much sleep over. If you were black, you better get over it now son.

Through every war movie and every novel the outcome is always the same. There is always a hero and there is always a villain. Which side one is on depends on which sets of ideology one believes in. It rolls over and over through history; the ideology practiced ritualistically spawns the birth of such credo.

This was a man made war with hypocritical rules. Citations for breaking the rules could never be on the right side of things. Life was life and only GOD could take away the breaths of the world's creatures. The flowers grew and the showers of spring fed the hills and the valleys. The seasons transformed with each passing moment in awe, as man trembled and marveled in appreciation at the most magnificent gift from the almighty. Paint a picture or tell a story. Speak the written word and share the tales passed down through the ages marking the moments of time on a line when we used those few fleeting moments we had to live, killing other human beings. Ron surrendered to his animal ego completely and ate with the rats in the company of darkness.

God had abandoned him. He'd switched over into the hell where God would not go. There were no chance encounters or coincidences of divine intervention. God stayed out of the fight letting the devil do his work. The light doesn't fight the dark. Only the dark can fight the dark. Chaplain Charlie the priest on the base was so shaken by the deaths and grisly wounds on the soldiers that he too wrapped his arm and drove the spike in clean. There was no plan for happiness. Even the priest could see that.

Chapter 11

Pete 'Killed in Action' – Vietnam, 1966

In 1965, Ron returned to the world burned out and destroyed. The skyscrapers of New York City towered over him once again; his mind flashing in and out of the jungle canopy. When a helicopter flew by in the city he stopped and looked for the tracer bullets shooting down the enemy. When the sirens blasted down the streets on a police car, his body pumped. In a big city full of lights he found himself lost in a concrete jungle with another unfamiliar enemy. He was on another level. The friendly streets he knew as a child no longer existed. The past corridors were shrouded in the shadows of dismay leading him back to nowhere; to the memories of his father and brother that were taken from him.

Ron could not face his mother. He had spoken to her from overseas and in his state of mind, he could still hear the concern in her voice when she asked if he was all right.

"That last picture you sent?"

"Yes."

"The one where you're with a couple of other gentlemen in the field?" she asked.

"Yes."

"The one picture. Those things around your neck, Ronnie?"

They were ears. Ron cut the ears off the faces of his victims. He strung them on a line and wore them around his neck. The putrid stink of rotting flesh hung half on the inside of his shirt decayed and black. When there was nothing to do and the faces of lifeless corpses danced in their heads, they played cards. They used the ears of dead Viet Cong for poker chips and he'd never thought about it until she asked him. And post traumatic stress disorder took hold.

"You mother fucker." Ron grabbed the hand by the wrist and pulled the arm through the light in the darkness cursing at the arm that was now bleeding.

"I'll fucking kill you." He did not care. He screamed and the arm screamed. But Ron would not let the wrist go until he torqued the elbow hard, wrapping his legs around the shoulder, breaking the arm. He finally released the grip when he had done all the damage he wanted so he could prove some kind of a point, but no one cared about it in the darkness. The voice on the other side of the light screamed out as it faded away.

Ron was left with only the darkness for 30 days and 30 nights in a fecal detention of vomit and urine. The beard on his face was caked in the muck of excrement.

"Who are you?"

His wind bubbled up in a tonic of dementia throwing his life around and he left his eyes open. Bambi was drinking from a stream with Thumper in a make believe cartoon. He hunted Yosemite Sam furiously through the desert on a horse in the blazing sun. He grew delirious with no sleep and then too much of it. The jungle made him an alert animal, indiscretion in disguise; sleeplessness into the gateways of schizophrenia. Back in the thick at least he could behave like an animal in whatever chaos the last apocalypse had exposed. The stories told throughout history were true about the Vietnam War. There were no heroes except the ones who lived. There was nothing heroic about the effort used and in the end, half a generation of young American men were dead or so wasted there was no return; indiscriminately slaughtered and ground into round piles, with the worms at the end of decay and rot.

There were no friends, only foes. Human life was so frail, the image played freely into the alternative justification. Most little boys play cowboys and indians or cops and robbers in the woods and build forts. The age of innocence eludes them, stealing seconds of their happiness as they develop their minds and find their own identities. In school the question is always, 'What do you want to be when you grow up?' Always the question demanded of youthful aspirations. Most kids say, 'President of the United States', 'Banker' or 'Lawyer'. Ron knew early that he only wanted to be a Marine.

Boot camp, Marine Corp, the draft…you went to Vietnam or you died trying. Children play with sticks and feathers and bows and arrows. Marines don't play. They kill and they killed everything they saw: the virtual reality of drug induced battle fatigue. They were zombies with M16's and hand grenades. Search and destroy. Blow up everything in a 30 kilometer radius and fry it with napalm.

Ron spun the dials for the incoming coordinates on the map. The barrel of the Howitzer rotated around to its direction and adjusted for its arc ready to pin up the stitches of enemy Viet Cong across the border 15 miles into Cambodia; the timeout for Viet Cong recruits and the road stop on the highway to napalm and storms of Agent Orange; the poisonous lethal fertilizer sucked the life from every living thing it contacted. The two together were modern warfare on its most psychopathic levels eating through the flesh while burning a hot brand as it sizzles down to the bone and not even the deepest oceans or coldest snows can stop it.

Chapter 12

Pete in Vietnam one week before his death

Ron's only escape from the pain was to embrace the future. He took a step away from all of the past for a moment when I met him. I had to pull him back to the kind loving person who I saw when I first met him. Forgiveness and creation given away freely to everybody. I pass the spliff to Ron to light while he tells me his story. We smoked the Dutch Moroccans I rolled up and we were best friends; all of us. He made us believe what we ourselves did not have the courage to believe could be possible. Not all people are superhuman. Ron Van Clief however, is.

Ron was the chief instructor for the black belts in the Ruiz dojo. In 1971 Urban told him to create his own style because he was as good as the rest of the instructors - if not better. When he trained with Ruiz, he had to drop his rank under Ruiz to brown belt. The demoralization made him work harder and he became the best fighter in the school. He had to fight for position. They were like dogs in a cage with no thought of the consequences of breaking open a man. Ruiz was a 5'6" Puerto Rican who retired undefeated at the age of fifty. The time and space reality of hand to hand combat began to take on an art form all its own. Ruiz was a decorated Korean War veteran and a United States Marine. He ruled the dojo like a fire team.

Ron was a living legend and those of us who were graced by his presence are all the better for it. He took us back to the beginning where we saw all we ever wanted, hanging on the mobile as we lay speechless in the cradle; screaming, crying, wet and coughing and gagging on the birth of our own sarcophagus.

The movie of Ron Van Clief would be written by a sociopathic, sub-categorized lunatic, sub-categorized genius. In the eye of the spotlight one faithful teardrop away from the point of its opposite inflection, spinning away into the universe.

I had no choice but to go in as an undercover investigator. I had to portray the true essence of life in the south; the riots and the hate, the publicity of the KKK and the fear over the many millions of people who belonged to that despicable organization. Grandfathers and great-grandfathers lost so much more in those generations wasted on Gettysburg. In the noble response of fiction it is necessary to describe the vocabulary of the thousands of years written on our history. Let the poets decide. Let the artists create. How many movie stars had a spike in their arm? How many of ye all do not blow up the nose as it goes?

Unemployment was Ron's first disappointment upon arriving home. He stood all day in a line at the New York State Employment Office wrapping around two blocks of downtown Manhattan. The sun beat down and the women fanned themselves with one hand and had their other hands on their babies. Ron didn't sweat a bead. He was calm and relaxed, at ease as the line slowly shifted closer and closer to the door over the course of the day.

In the afternoon he made it inside. The building had installed a new air conditioning system. Ron smiled relaxed and easy, then eventually was ushered into a room with a table and a stack of paperwork with a little government worker man wearing a peace sign on his breast peering back at Ron through narrow round rimmed spectacles.

"We are a city of order Mr. Van Clief. A society governed by laws and respect. There is no work for you in this city. We do not need baby killers behind the wheels of our buses. We do not need psychopaths behind the lines of our hamburger restaurants. You are a danger to society."

Ron was outraged. There was nothing to say. He would crush the tiny man in his fingers leaving the room in the state of a chicken slaughterhouse.

"You're telling me there are no jobs."

"Mr. Van Clief. You went to war to kill for the government of the United States. You are in violation of human rights and moral obligations to human kind. We will not have a killer like you on the loose with our children and our women. We have no need for machine gunners in civilian life."

But it was nothing new. He'd never been wanted in this world. He was trash that could be thrown away, that piece of cloth from a sack of rice that goes to the gutter when all has been eaten and everyone is full. Most people only think about the rice when they're eating it. They never think about the sack. In the orient, fishermen used those sacks sewn together to make sails for their boats. Ron was wrapped with so many dirty sacks he didn't care anymore for the taste of rice. He didn't care for the taste of anything anymore. His mouth went bland.

He went to the Veteran's Hospital to find an answer and they told him he suffered from Post Traumatic Stress Disorder as if he didn't already know. There were new pharmaceuticals sprouting up in the psychiatric testing laboratories. Dr. Slessinger assured him they would cure his mind of the horrors and nightmares allowing him to function adequately in a postmodern society.

"Do you think you are God?"

"I do not think I am God. I said I'm bullet proof."

"You're saying you can't be killed?"

"Everyone gets killed. They're killing us every day. But they haven't got to me and they never will. Out there..." Ron's mind flew off to the clouds swooping in low on a burning village. "When you're flying," he continued. "And you're strapped in. The boys put a syringe in your arm and you're flying. Nothing can stop you. Nothing can touch you."

"Didn't you get shot down?"

"That's not the point. I pulled guys out of the shit and onto that chopper before I could see I only had the torso in my hands. The legs were left somewhere else in the grass. All I have are dog tags. Their faces turned to paste and their skin is cold like clay and they start to rot and I am not rotting." He flexed his muscles and stood up.

"I see Corporal. You are a very impressive man," Dr. Slessinger said tapping his pen on his paper pad. "Tell me, do you ever see yourself with a rifle in the streets of the city perhaps?"

"I don't know. That's all I see." And that's all he saw in his mind as I pried inside.

95

"How do you feel talking about it?"

"It's not easy."

"I will help you find some closure."

"There is no closure. How can there be closure? I killed people because the captain told me to shoot these fuckers; women, kids, whoever."

"But come on. You are an inspiration for so many people today," I said.

"Have you ever had to kill anyone?"

"No, of course I haven't"

"Then you don't know what I'm talking about."

"I don't."

"Should I define it better because I don't think you're getting what I'm saying? When I came back from Vietnam I thought I was ok. I didn't want to be debriefed. I didn't want to be psychoanalyzed. I didn't want any of it. They put me through some of it anyway. Decades later, there's no closure. They can put me on whatever drugs they want to but it changes nothing. Those things happened. That can't change. My brother got killed at 22 years old. How can that change? You can't just say it was 35 years ago and be done with it. The brain doesn't work that way. Anybody who was in the shit will tell you the same. Ask the republican who ran for president. You don't think John McCain still has bad dreams? The Viet Cong tied his hand behind his back and suspended him from a rope until his shoulder dislocated. They took it down and did it again the next day. They told him he could go home but he refused because he was the senior commanding officer in Hilton Hanoi. He suffers from a disorder many captured prisoner's face. After being tortured so long you eventually start to agree with your captor so the beatings will stop."

"That's why he shouldn't be in that position", Dr. Slessinger said.

"He would be the worst president in history because when your mind is so twisted in the first place, you can't differentiate from then and now. You can't. He wouldn't be a good president because the guys who have seen that much have lost their feelings. For decades I didn't give a shit about anything else except my kids. I didn't even give a shit about any of the wives. I've only cared about my children and my students. I blacked out everything else. The rest of the world did not exist anymore. That was for decades. Can you imagine decades?"

"I've only been imagining for less than decades."

Ron painted himself into a corner. He was a black marine in Vietnam with a uniform. One day he looked in the mirror and asked, "Who the fuck are you?" He would not excuse himself for his misconduct in the service. He could not excuse it by saying that he was ordered to do it, because life is precious. The things he did made him guilty.

All the shrinks in the world could say everything but he'd heard it all. He would be in therapy for 37 years under twelve different psychiatrists. Three of them were Vietnam vets and the guys that would try to help him were dead now. Half had blown their brains out and the other half had self-induced toxicosis. Dr. Killebrew fell over dead of a heart attack when he came face to face with the past. He was an Air Force pilot who'd been shot down in Korea and went through the same POW shit as McCain. He was Ron's therapist and helped with the deprogramming. They would try to erase it but they never could. Every time Ron spoke to his shrink, he asked if it would ever get better. Would it ever change? There was no better. There was only coping.

"That is not all the world is Ron," Dr. Killebrew said. "You did a great service to your country and the American people. Your country owes you a deep gratitude for your patriotism and sacrifice. I want to start you on a prescription of Carisoprodol to calm things down a bit. It should help you sleep. It does for most people. I'm also going to give you a prescription for tranquilizers if you can't sleep. And if you suffer any manic episodes on the Carisoprodol, I'm writing a prescription for some antidepressants. I think this is a good cocktail that should have you back on the right track before too long."

Chapter 13

The summer of '65, Ron took a walk in examination for the Transit Police Department. The Police Academy was a joke. Policemen were not trained to sufficiently deal with modern criminals. His knowledge of aggressive behavioral control far surpassed anything taught in the hand on hand combat manual of the New York City Police Department. They welcomed him because he stood so straight in a uniform. He passed the test with ease. His veteran credentials put him at the top of the list. He wanted to be the perfect cop. His captain was Lew Alcindor, the father of basketball star Kareem Abdul Jabbar. Captain Alcindor disliked Ron and wrote him up for minor things like missing a button. Captain Alcindor didn't like Ron's afro stuffed into his uniform cap.

His on duty hours were 8 p.m. to 4 a.m. on the infamous D train. He rode the D train from Coney Island to the Bronx. On any given tour of duty, he would see at least two assaults and robberies. The other cops thought he was too active in the arrest and summons department with Miranda rights. His mind was keyed for the jungle and he adapted it to the step of an inner city policeman. He'd been trained to spot out the unordinary. He jumped at every thief and crook he crossed paths with. He booted out the bums who pissed on the doors of the train. He cleared the junkies out of the bathrooms in the tunnels. He cleared the riffraff who spoke disgustingly to middle class folks on their way home from a long day's work. He was a beacon of light.

But still, Vietnam left Ron with a disillusioned perspective of the disorganized manner of the police department and the judicial system. All the courts did was tie up money from the taxpayers to make the lawyers rich. He would arrest someone for armed robbery in the morning then see them on the street before he got off duty later that evening. There was no room in the jail cells for junkies and thieves that could not be fed when they wouldn't eat anyway and would rather claw at the walls until their fingers bled and then released back to sniff out their next fix.

Each tour of duty was its own mission. Ron's mission was to go home in one piece; no different than in the thick. The New York subway system was a jungle made of concrete with shadows, corners and eyes lurking everywhere. The speech of foul odor breathed on the mosaic tile corridors where homeless people slept and kids who shot smack died before their 19th birthdays.

Ron rekindled his obsession with the peacemaker of the Wild West determined to live out the lifestyle of John Wayne. He carried a revolver in his holster and drew it so much that the leather fit soft and smooth on the hammer when he put the catch back on. He spit shined his shoes as he did in the military. He'd joined the department to make a difference and he wondered if things could work out that way.

The tour started off as usual at the district office. There was roll call and the officers went to their posts. Some cops had a particular post while others covered several stations. The subway noise was deafening. It was a Friday night and the trains were crowded. The weight of humidity condensed in thick fog on the windows. Some of the cars on the D train were air conditioned, some weren't.

It was early and Ron could feel the sweat rolling down his back beneath his bulletproof vest. He didn't normally wear the vest because of its awkward burden. He started his patrol at the front of the train. The motorman and the conductor were on the train platform. Stillwell Avenue was a giant station filled with people coming and going from Coney Island.

As the door closed, several of his police buddies waved at him. He checked the time on his watch and made some entries in his log book. The train was packed with sunbathers returning after a long day of drinking and smoking their minds out. The subway car was packed full of kids blasting music from their tape recorders. He knew it was going to be one of those nights. The hairs on the back of his neck were already riled up from a few lines of coke he did in the bathroom stall at the last stop. He always took something to keep him alert on the job. He wouldn't be caught sleeping.

Slowly he made his way through the train car. By the time the train reached the next station he needed some fresh air away from the smell of salt and sand and the rank of ingested alcohol and vomit from adolescent mischief. He stuck his head out the door and waved to the conductor. The conductor left the door open so that Ron could make it into the next car. At every station stop Ron got out at the platform and went to the next subway car. The train roared to the next station. His eyes looked over every inch of each subway car. He jumped all the cars many times on his rounds to the Bronx searching every one of them. His persistence was deliberately habitual, hopped up on juice, blow and smoke. The sounds of the train running beneath his feet on wheels of steel and sparks in the darkness of the shadows from the windows passed with every turn in the tunnels. Music played in his brain of a distant bell or whistle blowing, a pop and a drum beat for every step of his patrol. He was alone. He'd ridden the train right out of hell and back under the streets of New York City's spellbinding mischief while enforcing the law.

He was a popular face and honorable people saw that Ron was a good choice to protect the community. In his enormous swagger of authoritative vigilantism he precluded himself from being the hero that never was.

On one stop an elderly lady became caught in the doors. She was being dragged down by the train along the subway platform. Ron rushed to the door and pulled her into the subway car. She was not injured. At the next stop she raced out the door and Ron continued his patrol with a nod of his cap, lifted eyebrow and flatline stare. The conductor laughed and shook his head.

Ron was ice. He practiced martial arts every day to develop his own style of Chinese Goju and it was yet another focus to strain him during the working hours of the D train. Another vice to test his disciplines of perseverance.

The D train was approaching the first stop in Manhattan. Ron's face was numb from a couple bumps he did off in the bathroom at the last stop. The train would start to thin out there. By the time Ron reached the Bronx it would be one quarter full. The trip from Coney Island to the Bronx took about two hours and he needed the extra jolt to go back into the darkness. The shift seemed like twenty hours and sometimes ran underground with the haunting of a solitary closing, confining him to inches of space. Ron flew through the train as though his steps were replaced by the air outside of the train passing by him like a flash of vampire between glimmering sunlight. Here he rode his metal snake beneath the city on the hunt for rats skipping holes in the field.

Ron glanced at two undercover cops when he scanned his next car. They were members of the pickpocket squad. He left them without word moving to the next car. The most effective weapon a policeman has is visibility. Just being on the scene deters criminal action. Ron wanted to be an undercover cop hoping to observe criminals in the absence of paranoia and sobriety of the uniform. He tore off his metaphysical shirt and was hopped up on Mescaline flitting through pages of his comic book characters. The world became a marshmallow of echoing trance mixed with the prescriptions of uppers and downers. He had meds for the pain and meds for the sadness. Mixed with a spoonful of Mescaline in your coffee, it broke it all down.

Several skinheads kicked the door as the train opened at the stop before Manhattan. Ron looked at them and the skinheads looked back. One kid with a Mohawk haircut spit on the window. Ron smiled at what to him seemed a very normal thing, having been out of the country. They rolled on. The next stop was Times Square: 42nd St. Station. Times Square had become a homeless shelter for the worst of transient discards in its recent years. When the train stopped, Ron looked to see how many cars to the engine. He'd been on the train for a long time this day.

He spotted a young Latino from the corner of his eye running past him closely pursued by the two undercover cops. The kid ran up the stairs and into the crowd of people. Ron used his radio to call the station cop who caught the fleeing Latino pickpocket at the top of the stairs. By the time the doors closed again on the D train, the station cop was handcuffing the young man. The two undercover cops looked surprised. As the train pulled away, Ron could see the undercover cops smacking the Latino kid across the face and the station cop walking away.

With a fresh load of weirdoes and vagrants, the train roared out of Times Square back in the direction it came from. Ron had to take a fresh breath as the train cleared again into the open city. The smells crawled through his nose and when he saw a homeless man urinating on one of the doors, he smacked him with his club, escorting him off the train at the next platform threatening to break his arm just as he'd broken the arm from the window of light in the darkness in the belly of the whale.

The outlandish charades of the D train were comical in comparison to his years in the war. His heightened state put him in survival mode. The contrasts and similarities between the life of the Marine Corp and the civilian life of a D train transit cop were surreal. Ron reached a sense of separation between the two and with it a vision of enlightenment, completely aware of all his surroundings. Though he was aware, it did not make the task of burying the past any easier. But because he could recognize the two worlds, he found it only in the conscious road that was set for him alone. His altered sense of euphoria was a direct result of the brain medications accelerating his hypomania. The medications in addition to the coke were enough to fly to the moon. He was ready to go if he could jump high enough. He would strap himself to a rocket if he hadn't already strapped himself to the gun bird.

He lived at his mother's house during these days. When he first returned from Vietnam it took him 7 months to contact her. She told Ron she was afraid of him. He was not the same son that left five years ago. The trauma and the drugs left him in a world he was too ashamed to show her. New York City had become a haven for junkies and gang violence had heated up. It was always the city it had been but now there was also a population on needles and pill addiction in the absence of mind to stop at nothing short of both injuring themselves while causing harm to others. The concrete jungle locked him inside his own bedroom when he was not training at the academy or working around for hustle.

He had a revolver and a baton. Nothing was a scene after landmines and disembowelment on the battlefield. The duality conflict split his personality even further. He attempted to recover from the stress under battle, but he never would, shaking it off in the mirror as he practiced his Clint Eastwood draw in the bathroom in all of his spare time. When he blew a hole in Doris' bedroom wall, she kicked him out.

Ron carried his gun upside down in the holster like *I Spy*. He could do anything he wanted to. The other cops hated him because he was overzealous. But he knew the criminal court procedure and he did the same thing he did in the military.

As the train pulled out of the station, Ron stuck his head out the window again to see a man jump the turnstile on the subway platform. He was headed for the door where Ron was standing. When he entered, Ron spun him around. The conductor watched the station cop rushing to his assistance. Suddenly, the 'flare jumper' pulled a straight razor and slashed out at Ron's left wrist leaving a gash and blood spurting everywhere.

Ron kicked the man hard in the groin and as the jumper fell back the razor dropped to the ground. There was a dash for the blade but then the station cop fired two rounds into the criminal's body and he fell into a heap on the floor of the train car. Ron looked over his shoulder to see the station cop in a kneeling position holstering his weapon. The rookie cop had shot the man after the razor was already on the ground. Ron called a stop to the train. The rookie cop stood paralyzed in fear on the subway platform watching the man spasm, kicking his feet in the air from his gunshot wounds like a decapitated chicken. Ron was bleeding out too. The razor chipped his wrist bone severing his tendons and ligaments. An ambulance was called for and rushed the two of them to the emergency room where Ron was given stitches and the man's life was saved.

The wounded turnstyle jumper had mugged a woman at the top of the stairs of the subway. After three months of going back and forth in the justice system, he was found guilty. He was sentenced from seven to fifteen years for felonious assault, robbery, fare evasion and resisting arrest. Two years later, Ron saw him in Times Square. They both nodded and went their separate ways. That was the story on the street. It didn't matter the corruption inside the police force was bad, the justice system couldn't afford the cleanup. His job wasn't to kill people or put bad people in jail. His job was to act as a public masseuse fondling the erogenous appetite of sociopathic outbursts allowing them to quell at their own expedience or be brought to such calming compassionate compromise.

Ron's days as a transit cop became another lesson in modern Zen psychotherapy. He was still a black man in a uniform. His superiors were still demeaning and bigoted. There was always something to prove between ranks and so much red tape to do it. The gaping wounds of disorder within the police department could never be covered. Black cops were harder on black prisoners than the racist white cops were for the very reason it took that much more to become a successful black man. Older men were trying to teach younger men respect.

One day eight policemen were beating a prisoner handcuffed to a radiator. Ron's mind passed over the scene as though it was a little girl buying candy from the grocers. The beating was nothing new for him. He carried on his way and as his shift ended, he prepared for his next job as a bouncer.

Chapter 14

DEPARTMENT OF THE TREASURY
UNITED STATES SECRET SERVICE
FILE

ROOM 623
6 World Trade Center
New York, N.Y. 10048-0963
Telephone: 212-466-4400

November 10, 1988

Kyoshi Ronald Van Clief
P.O. Box 359
Ansonia Station
New York, New York 10023

Dear Kyoshi Ronald Van Clief,

On behalf of the many Agents of the U.S. Secret Service you
successfully trained in the Martial Arts, I would like to take this
opportunity to extend our deepest gratitude for your efforts.

The comprehensive program you developed enabled the Agents to
achieve a pratical and profound knowledge of self-defense tactics
incorporating both the mental and physical aspects of the Martial
Arts. The progress we achieved was no doubt a result of your patience,
knowledge and understanding of the interaction which is needed between
the student and the instructor.

Once again we would like to extend our deepest thanks for
imparting your knowledge and expertise which will stay with us always
and enable us to perform our law enforcement duties in a safe and confident manner.

Yours, truly,

Ronald A. Patell
Special Agent

**Ron Van Clief Senior Defensive Tactics Instructor at the World Trade
Center, New York City (1983-1993)**

The Electric Circus was the best disco in the East Village
on St. Mark's Place. The EC housed all the great performers of
the time like Sly and the Family Stone, The Chambers
Brothers, Chicago, Earth, Wind and Fire, Santana and The
Rolling Stones. Ron puffed tough with Jimi Hendrix. He was a
rock star. Jimi could drink like the ocean swallow's fleets of
fishing boats and he could fuck so that none of those fishing
boats would ever come home again to a lonely maiden.

Chaka Zulu was head of security. Zulu is the reincarnation
of the legendary African warrior chief. He was savage enough
since his role in the movie where he would wake up every
morning and pick one of his family members to be killed;

skewered on a spike and posted at the gate of the kraal alongside the others asserting the ultimate prowess of authority. Zulu hired Ron to work with him as security. The minimum requirement for the team was a black belt level in martial arts. They trained together every day before work in Chinatown at Grand Master Peter Urban's dojo. Peter Urban was the founder of Goju Karate which made him the equivalent to George Washington in the martial arts world in America. Peter broke through bricks and boards with his hands, feet and head. He floored guys three times his size. He mastered all of the weapons. In 1962, he'd beaten Don Nagle in a legendary performance. All of the bouncers learned from Peter Urban. They practiced together religiously after hours at the Circus with a few lines of invincibility in them.

The Circus was a psychedelic trip with flashing lights and a mega sound system that rocked the house. It was home to Andy Warhol and the velvet underground that put neon paintings all around to morph out on hallucinogens, projected movies and photographs simultaneously. The experience was called the 'Exploding Plastic Inevitable'.

Drugs and booze went rampant at the Circus and the hippy culture formed to protest the Vietnam War. Hippie kids passed out and crashed out in the Pillow Room. The Pillow Room was where they smoked pot and played around. The hippies didn't bother anybody too much. The trippers were no problem unless they were on some bad LSD or strong PCP. They'd shoot up peanut butter to see if it got them stoned. They mostly had sex in big orgies and danced the whole night to loud music. The real trouble was throwing out the drunks. The bikers created the worst combination of everything.

Ron was next to Zulu in command and then there was Malachi Lee, Tom LaPuppet, Owen Watson, Fred Hamilton, Ronald Taganashi, Grandmaster Frank Ruiz and Earl Monroe; a mission impossible team nobody wanted to mess with. By the year 2009 all the above mentioned masters would be dead leaving only Ron and Zulu alive. One particular night a bunch of bikers crashed the door. Bob Chin, Ron's dojo brother was arguing with a big biker. Ron knew Bob had no patience at all. He would floor the guy quickly and the place would erupt in a brawl of knives and chairs, maybe even shots fired. The music was so loud Ron couldn't hear what was being said. Bob's facial expressions told the whole story. The bikers surrounded him closing in for the kill. Bob kicked the biker in the groin. By the time Ron joined in several of the other bouncers were there. Malachi Lee, towering seven feet tall, ran over and slipped on something wet, falling like a giant timber.

The biker with an iron cross tattooed across his skull pulled out a knife heading for Malachi. Malachi rose from the ground knocking him flat on his back with a kick in the face. Chaos and pandemonium ensued. Ron Taganashi jumped in the air with a flying side kick, breaking the jaw of another biker with the tattoo of a leprechaun pissing in an empty pot with flames shooting out of his prick. As the biker staggered backwards he was kicked in the stomach by Louie Delgado, the All American champion who studied with Bruce Lee. Louie had no mercy with anyone. He practiced his kicks and punches on the patrons at the Electric Circus. If people were getting rowdy in the least he'd check them.

Now all the bouncers and bikers were brawling as if it were the Klondike westerns with a symphony of voice over's from a Kung Fu movie and the vocals of a rock band wailing through the floors. The bikers were thrown out into the street before anybody realized what had happened. Ron snapped the leprechaun's arm behind his back until it broke and launched him through the bakery window across from the Circus.

Sly and the Family Stone were setting up their equipment on the stage and barely took notice. The fight was over. Zulu and Ron went to the kitchen for something to eat. Bob Chin was there with two hippie chicks using the counter space like the backseat of a car. Zulu and Ron made their food and bounced after a little encouragement from Bob's girls.

They strolled cool around the premises. Ron had his hair puffed out in a bouncy afro and wore bell bottom jeans and boots during the day. They climbed the stairs to the balcony. There were ten slide projectors and lasers on the crowd shining down a myriad of colors and lights flashing over 10,000 square feet and several thousand people. The Rolling Stones packed in six thousand to the door.

Cleo Davies was the only woman bouncer on staff. She was a combination of all top five Miss America candidates wrapped into one and shooting the moon with cunning. She was one of Zulu's black belt student/girlfriends at the Nisei Goju dojo. Cleo had the courage and cunning of a lioness. She'd kicked two biker chicks in the face with a double high kick. The second girl was on her knees by the time the first one hit the floor. She was the best woman fighter in New York at the time.

Everybody trained all day and hung out at the Circus at night. Sex, drugs and rock 'n roll were the order of the day. Zulu, Ron and Owen Watson trained ever so diligently with Sensei Urban and went to tournaments every month. Their personalities differed making them a fearsome trio. Owen Watson was ruthless. He was a great fighter in and out of the ring. Owen was a ladies' man. He had the biggest ego and thought he was a Chinese warlord. Though he was a maniac, he still dedicated himself to the world of martial arts. The three of them trained together for seven years. Together, they developed the Chinese Goju system and worked to bring in the top fighters around America.

Ron bounced back and forth between the Electric Circus and The Dom. The Dom was the best black night spot in New York. It was below the Electric Circus. The DJ's were the best. When the clubs upstairs and around the city were full, the basement at the Dom was full of blacks rocking their socks.

The whites stayed upstairs at the Electric Circus. Ron felt better at The Dom. It was a dance crowd and Ron liked to dance, jamming out on the hot disco music pumping all night on the heavy sound system.

Tom LaPuppet and Ron worked back and forth between The Dom and Electric Circus for three years during which time Tom opened up Ron's mind to verbalization. Instead of resorting to physical violence they would utilize their vocabulary and communication skills to diffuse potentially dangerous situations. One night Tom talked a brother out of his gun that he was pointing at Ron. Zulu and Ron's religious devotion to Nisei Goju became baptismal. They sparred on the sixth floor roof on the edge of the ledge practicing balance and coordination. They almost fell off every time.

Sensei Ruiz ran the Nisei Goju Dojo. He would pit each of the black belts against other black belts. That made interesting matches for sparring. In the old days the students were devoted like in the Chinese movies. The students trained under the knowledge that there was always somebody out there working harder than they were and the only way to beat them was to work harder.

The martial arts world was not prone to drugs, however there were women everywhere; groupies in every color imaginable. It was not uncommon for Zulu and Ron to share them. Orgies were commonplace at the East Village walk up. In the 1960's the East Side began to develop its own culture and became known as the East Village. Scores of artists and hippies began to move into the area, attracted by the base of beatniks that had lived there since the 1950's. Zulu and Ron would take women back to their apartment and drop hits of sunshine acid in their drinks, and then have sex while the ceiling melted.

The marijuana odor inundated the apartment; a three room railroad style flat with a bath tub in the kitchen next to the sink.

The place was tiny, but they would pack it with three or four women at a time. As a policeman, Ron would come home at different hours during the night. Zulu always had someone in bed when he came home. They had hundreds of girlfriends. AIDS wasn't around in the 1960's so everybody was doing everybody in a sexual free for all.

Owen Watson was a real ladie's man. He had more women than all of them and they were all exquisite in some form. He was a party animal. He was a great fighter but had a lot of mental hang-ups which kept him from being good in competitions. He was ultra-violent: violent to the 10th degree type. He kicked and hit women as hard as he hit men. He was a sadist and an ogre, yet there was an almost likeable side to him. Ron and Owen became dojo rivals.

It was Owen who invented the electric pipe with the hose and face mask; like going into a gas chamber but the gas was inside the mask. The gas mask covered the nose and exposed the mouth. The smoke would travel up your nose and out of the mouth. The sensation was overwhelming. Everyone laughed when someone would hit the floor after five minutes with the mask. The lenses were lavender which enhanced the hallucinogenic effect of the weed they smoked. It had variable pump levels which Owen would increase as the person wearing the mask started to inhale. Owen knew he was evil.

He practiced black magic and witchcraft along with his martial arts training. Owen's students were actually covert disciples in his secret cult. One of them stabbed Ron with a knife through his right wrist. The student confessed to Ron that Owen made him do it. Ron would have to sort things out. He played Owen's students in a three on one sword play where the students tried to hack away at Ron's limbs. By this point, however, Ron was a skilled swordsman. With a samurai sword, he could snap a carrot on your larynx and not even touch the skin. The students were choking on the floor before their swords could pose.

Sensei Ruiz was in charge under Sensei Urban and he liked to keep the static going between the hispanics and blacks. On Tuesday nights they would have the black belt class at Nisei Goju. Sensei Ruiz would teach the class. The students would form two lines facing each other and start fighting. Everyone would fight everyone. Sensei Ruiz picked out his victims individually. Ron was always one of the privileged to be chosen.

One particular night Sensei Ruiz was on fire, chopping everyone in the line down one by one. He was a short stocky man who didn't look like much but could punch holes through walls with the tips of his fingers. After giving Owen a real beating, it was Ron's turn. Ron thought he was ready for him, but Sensei Ruiz had other ideas. He lunged at Ron hitting him in the face with a left reverse punch that rocked Ron so hard he stumbled. Ron shook it off and started his attack. Ron could see Owen and Zulu laughing over Sensei Ruiz's shoulder as if they knew what was going to happen next.

Ron kicked the sensei with a round kick that bounced off his chest. Sensei Ruiz just smiled and adjusted his black sunglasses. He wore the sunglasses when he was in a serious mood. Suddenly Ron was struck by a bolt of lightning. He saw the bright light that comes before death. When he woke, Sensei Ruiz stood over him whipping his face with a wet towel that brought him back to consciousness. Ron had been struck in the back of the head with a spinning back kick. He lay back on the mat clearing the cobwebs from his head embarrassed in front of the rest of the class and the great Sensei Ruiz.

The black belts fought each other routinely. There were a few scrapes and bruises, a few broken bones, but the one man Ron feared the most was Earl Monroe. Earl was Zulu's age, six years older than Ron himself. He'd broken five of Ron's ribs on two separate occasions. Earl was the enforcer of the team. He was a practitioner of Judo and Jiu Jitsu with lots of real life experience as a bouncer. Earl was the toughest fighter in the dojo. It took Ron three years to control the fear he had of Earl Monroe. They became brotherly and led each other to the rank of senior black belts. They ruled Nisei dojo with an iron fist building a disciplined army for Sensei Ruiz.

Chapter 15

THE BLACK DRAGON
poster in 1974

In the summer of 1969 Ron won his first World Karate Championship in the Japan Expo at the New York Coliseum. He took first place in the middleweight division and second place in Black Belt Kata. He lost to Louis Delgado; who took on Chuck Norris in earlier rounds.

Chuck at the time had trained in Korea in the art of Tang Soo Do. He was a smart fighter who thought of his opponent's mind, playing on his personality rather than his movements. Louis was an amazing fighter; tough as nails with a sledge hammers for arms. Louis threw one of his classic front kicks and Chuck side stepped him sweeping Louie's supporting leg. As Louie fell to the floor, Chuck punched him in the face with a textbook uppercut. The fight would launch Norris into becoming one of the finest point fighters of his generation.

Ron entered over 400 tournaments and garnered over 500 trophies. He became the chief instructor of the Nisei Goju black belt classes in sparring and self-defense and shortly after trained his recruits at the King's Highway Karate Academy. His coworkers at the Electric Circus were now his disciples. After class they would go to Music Palace Theatre in Chinatown to watch movies. While sitting in the audience watching *The Boxer from Shantung*, it hit him. He knew he could do it. He knew he could take on the world. He practiced harder and trained seven hour days, seven days a week. One day Harry Madsen showed up to class. He was the Vice President of the East Coast Stuntmen's Association. Their friendship was established and so began Ron's movie career.

When he became friends with Richie Havens, Ron started doing even more acid and hallucinogenics. Ron and Richie put tablespoons of Mescaline in their coffee in the morning and smoked spliffs walking downtown back and forth between the Electric Circus and their apartments. They always smoked on the walk; nobody cared. It was the thing to do. One day they were walking through the park in Thompson Square. It was a beautiful fall morning. The birds were singing and the sky was full of clouds floating when the leaves started to grow on the backs of Ron's pupils. A man was playing a classical acoustic masterpiece on the guitar. The shadows in the trees looked around from their swelling eyes that were so sleepy from the passing time of idle solitude. The buds on the branches began to open up and flower before him. Chords of graduation climbed up the stairway to heaven in a psychedelic skip. A crowd of people gathered around, girls with flowers in their hair and young men with beards and sunshine in their eyes. Ron and Richie joined the group and dropped hits of LSD. The man was Jimi Hendrix.

There was always coke lined up across record albums on the table. A professor at New York University was stacking up sheets of LSD like notes on the topic of infinite insanity. He was the founder of 'Tune in, turn on and drop out'. He was

Timothy Leary and his grand intervention took him to the forest in the middle of the night on a full moon with 100 people dosing their minds out on the Kool-Aid experiment. Ron was one of them. The music played for hours until the darkness of nothing except the full moon and then in the center of the dance floor a spotlight shined down. A voice declared the spot of rain for all one hundred trippers there in the middle of the woods as a drop they created— the alternate universe in the presence of a human being to be born as above, so below like the constellations spinning a bottle on end throwing the flower of life through the essence of their souls. The music stopped and the light went out and everybody walked away on a slide of reality.

The height of the summer brought 400,000 people from across the country. They drove for days in buses, vans, cars and trucks. They came with everything and left with nothing; bodies abandoned by the objects that bound them. It was a movement for something different. Ron Taganashi and Ron piled four girls into the back of the van on their way to Wood-stock. They ate full sheets of LSD and smoked a pound of marijuana. LSD was a wonder drug. When a girl drank two hits of Sunshine she would do anything. Everyone screwed everyone that moved. They called it 'peace'. No more wars and no more nightmares. The greatest musicians in the world assembled in a field in the northern part of New York and Woodstock happened. Dance to the music.

The music started and in little pockets around the countryside the Kool-Aid experiment spread out like a fog upside a mountain. The American dream was hard to realize at the time and the people used the Vietnam War to split the country apart. How could an American be missing an arm or a leg from a bullet or a bomb? Nobody wanted to sign up for that. They didn't want any part of it. They challenged the womb which gave them the life for which they felt no patriotism. The government had run amok betraying the people and their soldiers and the generation revolted on anarchy.

Woodstock was liberation. There were stoned women everywhere and their boyfriends were too crazy with the new drug they didn't know how to handle them. Ron's mind was sharp on LSD. He'd taken it while competing in the Japan Exposition. It slowed everything down and put his opponent in perspective drawing victory and a World Championship. At Woodstock, the people sang as one. Days went by and the shadows of the people who arrived, departed from the ones who remained, packing in another 400,000 wandering souls. In the center of the maze of madness, flowers and every psycho-hallucinogenic drug known to man stood Ron. They could feel his study on them and demanded that he sport for the crowd. Chaka was at the festival and they sparred over and over for hours and worthy opponents challenged Ron acting out the grace of mastering the body to the beat of the musician's instruments. Ron made his movement into a dance and one by one the crowd erupted into flying kicks and punches.

The years became a blur with every day rolling into the next. Ron dealt with his mind through practice and training and the stiff regimen of drugs, but the horror in Vietnam refreshed itself daily in a synaptic flash of brain seizures. He married a beautiful woman with exotic eyes and the loins of Arabian fairytales. They were in love with the adrenaline rush of debauched freedom growing in America. She rekindled his sense of belonging in New York and they dreamed of starting a family. He moved out of Zulu's and into a small apartment with the hopes of monogamy and the start of facing his own destructive drug abuse.

He'd used drugs to numb the pain. He snorted coke and smoked weed to forget the horror, keeping it bottled up deep down inside. But he couldn't bury it forever. He didn't pull his brother Pete off the battlefield, but he pulled out a lot of other guys who were torn to pieces sometimes without even their dog tags to claim them. All the bodies he saw began to show Pete's face on them. He slept on his side huddled in a ball with his hand on his pistol next to his chest. He woke in the night screaming and lost, the walls closed in on him musty, suffocating his breath, breaking him into the cold sweats that his body did pour out purging the toxic destruction induced over the better part of a decade.

He could never forgive himself for Pete's death and he lost his smile. When there was the glimpse of one it was never the same as it was before boot camp. Pete was the innocence that he could remember. He knew what he himself had done in Vietnam and he knew that Pete must have had it worse. He was the real airborne ranger that gets the game going to clear the way for the fifty thousand reinforcements coming in behind him.

Doris felt betrayed. The agony she pleaded with furrowed across her face. The telephone rang one day. The military was making a row over Pete's sacrifice to the country by awarding him the Purple Heart. Doris showed up to the media press conference where a Lieutenant stood in front of a podium. Doris was called up to accept the medal for her son. The cameras were flashing lights in her face snapping pictures. The Lieutenant told her to smile big for the camera as he shook her hand. Doris had a beautiful smile with a straight set of pearly whites. She could barely turn up the corners of her mouth, she was so sick to her stomach. She broke down in front of the cameras and cursed the military, throwing the certificate and the medal on the ground at the Lieutenant's feet. They'd killed her son and no medal could replace him.

Ron never had the chance to be a hero in the war. The bastards fixed him up too many times, keeping him from this fatal glory. The nocturnal haunting became so prevalent Ron began suffering from insomnia. He loaded one bullet and spun the cylinder on his service revolver putting a round somewhere inside as a gamble. He pulled the trigger on the .38 snubnose over and over to the sound of a click, taking his first breath waking up each time in a new life.

He'd dodged so many bullets in the rounds of Russian Roulette he played in Saigon to settle his debts with Papisan and clean his slate so he could pay for more Asian whores. He didn't care once Pete died. Ron could have died a thousand times already. The anxiety calmed into a psychotic gaze. There was nothing to live for. Happiness was an illusion.

He enrolled at the New York film school and excelled, drawing attention from his teachers who recommended him for behind the scenes extra work on the studio sets. He joined the Negro Ensemble where he met the greatest black entertainers in the world. He worked with George Benson, Richard Pryor, and Eddie Murphy and as a personal security agent specialist for Gregory Hines. He'd already known Ossie Davis, who helped him get accepted at the Negro Ensemble Company. Then he met Samuel Jackson on the set of *Car Wash*. Years later Ron would be his stunt photo double on the set of *Die Hard with a Vengeance*.

Ron immersed himself in the film industry, taking classes at the University of the Streets School for screenwriting and filmmaking. His life would be the perfect movie. He'd not only seen everything happening at the time, it revolved around him in a mirage of the past, present and future inside his own little sphere. He was making his own history. He wrote a number of scripts and ideas, putting pen to paper recreating the nightmares from the dreams the night before.

Chapter 16

The wild bunch!

Back at work on the D train, Ron was approaching the end of his shift. A rustle of wind blew through the papers littered on the platform of the subway station. The train was empty except for one old man who worked in Manhattan as a tailor for a business that held a storefront name for 175 years. He was always the last man on the train. Ron had spoken with him many times before. He had to make the transfer through Queens after the long hours in the city when he got off of work, then went to see his daughter for supper as had become their tradition since his wife of 56 years passed the year before. His family was knit with the bonds of concentration and he bore as his wife once did, the numbers on his wrist inscribed in an Auschwitz tattoo parlor.

Ron entered into the last car of the train for his last walk through on the last run of the night. As the train rolled on; flickering lights from outside the windows bending around corners rocked back and forth between the cities. He was tired and ready for the shift to end and looking forward to getting things going later at the Electric Circus.

He could see two cars ahead through the door window's opening. A man rose from his seat and was walking towards the front of the train. Ron stepped up his pace at the sign of life noticing that everything was fine as he continued his patrol. There was nobody else in the next few cars and as the train passed around a curve in the city on its last stop to the East Side of Brooklyn, Ron could see the man again through the windows of the doors between the trains. The perpetrator stood over the old man in the next car and pulled something from his coat. The old man raised his hands as Ron skipped into stride feeling the panicked movements.

As he passed through the door joining the cars together, the man who was standing turned around startled. The man brandished a pistol pointed in Ron's direction. Instinctively Ron did a full point draw from his holster, aiming and squeezing the trigger, packing two rounds into the man's chest.

The tailor turned his head to Ron looking back down at the man. His face was warm but his eyes were cold and as he rose on the last stop, his gait was unrestrained from the actions over the last moments. The train stopped and the doors opened. Ron watched the tailor as he turned his head and nodded a sign of gratitude.

The ambulance came but it was too late for the assailant. He was a junkie and nobody really cared, but in the courtroom the mention of post traumatic stress disorder weighed in favor of the prosecution and Ron was forced to resign from the police force. Less than a year later he was reinstated, however Ron realized that being a police officer was not a good way to live. He chose the way of the martial arts and resigned from the police department. Later that week, the Black Panther party detonated a bomb inside the Electric Circus injuring 15 people. Ron was unemployed.

Chapter 17

The age had begun for a new era of black people in film. Blaxploitation films started capitalizing on the novelty of an African American martial artist. Ron started showing up on all the sets working as a full time stunt man for the biggest stars, building blockbusters overnight.

Ron fought at Madison Square Garden in front of Bruce Lee. Bruce named him the 'Black Dragon'. Bruce saw Ron lose in the preliminaries and said he was cheated. The guy Ron lost to won the championship that year. And Bruce you ask? He never competed. He liked to walk around to the different black belts and study their techniques. Kung Fu masters never competed openly in tournaments. There were a few exceptions but most didn't. Some of their styles were heavy contact on the equivalent to what modern Mixed Martial Arts would be, on a hard wood floor without the six ounce gloves and no weight limits. They were doing MMA in the sixties before the term was ever invented. The techniques didn't just pop out of anywhere; they were simply commercialized later.

Ron and Bruce crossed swords a dozen times or so. Bruce was unlike anybody else Ron ever sparred. Bruce had a broken rhythm and was faster. He had more skills of blocking and countering as opposed to just blocking and going in. He beat Ron to the punch sixty to seventy percent of the time. Ron could get in but had to pay for it. Bruce was an exceptional fighter and trained grappling with Gene Labell.

Bruce talked Ron into auditioning for a part as a black kung fu star. Thousands of black martial artists came from around the country to audition and in the end Ron won the title to be the Black Dragon. He travelled to Hong Kong to star in five kung fu films as a feature motion picture figure.

He was a black movie star; the very first to headline in an action movie in Hong Kong. The scene was slick. Hong Kong was flashing and the streets were popping. He basked in the surge of attention soaking it up into his body along with everything that came with it, including addiction. Opium is a barbiturate and slows the heart, creating a euphoric relaxation and preoccupation. Coke is an amphetamine, a stimulant which speeds up the heart giving the user a motivational rush and a forked tongue that rambles. When Ron put the two together, the camera came out of the set and into his eyes. Everything he saw became all that there was.

Ron walked slowly and thought fast, reacting deliberately and with precision. The faces of the Chinese population sent him tripping on and off with the catalyst of post traumatic stress, masquerading a nightmare that chilled his spine between the laughter hardening his figure to an emotionless piece of fallen timber.

In the mind of a true martial artist there is a balance of yin and yang. Though not all philosophies call it specifically by that name, most can agree that there is a balance, polarity or opposites; a positive and a negative form of combination which balances the circle of life.

Martial arts in the Orient, is a way of life, not a hobby. The Chinese had defended themselves for thousands of years on basic hand to hand combat. They were superior in their manipulations of the human body, in pressure points and submission. The Japanese styles developed the best of the Chinese points. Together these styles brought forth the most proficient methods of self-defense ever known to man. The techniques and traditions of each style were passed down from generation to generation. It was the American soldiers fighting in Asia during the 20th century who brought back the teachings and practices of the living masters currently practicing the subject.

His dream had come true. He was starring in kung fu movies and training with Jackie Chan, Bruce Lee, Carter Wong, Leo Fong, Jason Pai Piao, Chan Goon Tai, Unicorn Chan, Chen Sing and Wang Yu. Sonny Chiba, Sue Shiomi and Kurata were his favorite Japanese stars.

The Black Dragon movie put martial arts' films on the map. The movie was shot on location in the Philippines under the director Sarafim Karalexis. The shooting schedule was twelve to fifteen hours a day and spanned over 40 working days. He'd never worked so hard in his life.

Jason Pai Piau played Tai, a farm boy in the Chinese countryside who spends his days plowing fields and playing with the water buffalo. He is a superb martial artist and is tested one day when his brother Shuvu Chi returns to the village in a silk suit with an ivory cigarette holder inlayed in gold. Shuvu Chi speaks of the riches to be found in the Philippines and is envied by everyone including his brother Tai. Shuvu and Tai fought every day as young boys and one day Tai declared that he would beat Shuvu, though they remained amiable about the engagements. Out of love for his older brother, Tai submits.

"One day maybe you can be successful like me." Shuvu says. "But I wouldn't bet on it." Shuvu loans his brother Tai the money to get to the Philippines and tells him that he better not come back until he's made his riches.

When Tai lands in the Philippines he is introduced to the city life and his first awakening to opium addiction. People are strung out in the streets from opium withdrawals. Their eyes are black and they shake uncontrollably. There is nothing he can do for any of them. As he goes along his way trying to make it in the city he is pick pocketed by another Chinese man who also came to the Philippines in search of riches and fame.

Tai takes in the pickpocket and pays for their room at a hotel. Tai gets a job in the shipyards the same day and starts making money. The hours are long and the workers are beaten. They carry heavy loads back and forth from the ships to the dockyard. One day when a man is beaten, Tai steps in his way to save his life. The guards don't appreciate their authority being challenged and so Tai is forced to fight the entire mob of shipyard goons. He humbly apologizes trying to excuse himself from the situation but in the end when he is provoked and there is no sign the goons will back down, he is forced to fight and through his demonstration shows that he is the superior fighter. The head of the shipping yard puts Tai in charge of the shipyard goons and without knowing what he's getting himself into, Tai signs a five year contract with the Mobster Mr. Ling.

Ron goes undercover as the Black Dragon working in cooperation with the Philippine government investigating the shipyards and Mr. Ling. There are daily stories in the newspaper of how Mr. Ling's shipyard mafia are smuggling in opium to supply the black market but nobody can prove it. The Black Dragon and his team of detectives are met with resistance as they face Tai and the goons in the shipyards. It is only when

Tai rescues a girl being sold into prostitution that he learns through her what Mr. Ling is doing. Tai tries to cancel his contract but because he cannot read, finds out that he is bound for the term with Mr. Ling and if he breaks it, will owe $100,000.

After several encounters with the Black Dragon, Tai is convinced that he must destroy his boss and seeks out the help of the Black Dragon and the Philippine government to topple the mob. The plot thickens when assassins are hired to eliminate Tai and the Black Dragon. One of the assassins sent to kill Tai is his own brother, Shuvu Chi. Shuvu Chi rapes and murders Tai's girlfriend while Tai is fighting off the guards at Mr. Ling's palace. The final showdown in the desert is a script pulled from a spaghetti western with frame by frame tension as the two brothers square off and Tai proves to his brother Shuvu once and for all he is the superior martial artist. Tai defeats his brother without killing him, leaving him disgraced and miserable in the desert.

Ron returned to Hong Kong with red carpet treatment. He was a VIP. Bruce Lee was excited about making the movie. *Fist of Fear, Touch of Death* which was the ultimate showdown in the Eastern hemisphere. The Black Dragon and the Dragon worked together again, this time Ron doing the choreography for the fights. They practiced sticky hands Kung Fu with Ron setting the choreography for all the fight scenes. Bruce Lee was portrayed as the bad guy. It was a major accomplishment for black people in the film industry. The super star kid of Asia was to be struck down and defeated in the world of martial arts.

The American public was thrilled to have one of their own duking it out on the Asian kung fu scene. Ron's style of Chinese Goju struck up conversations in the martial arts' world and with his accomplishments and World Championship under him, there was more excitement to keep starring this black anomaly in the Orient and negotiations for the *Black Dragon's Revenge* went to contract, scheduled to be shot later that year.

In the movie, Ron returned to the United States, living in San Francisco after working for the Filipino government. The following year he is hired by a gangster in Chinatown to fly to Hong Kong and investigate the death of Bruce Lee. The speculation of rumors ran rampant on the part of the martial arts world claiming that Bruce Lee overdosed on too much sex and too many drugs. Ron doesn't believe it, suspecting foul play. The moment Ron arrives in Hong Kong people are after him. On every street corner Ron finds himself surrounded by men who try to kill him. The closer Ron gets to finding out the identity of the murderer, the more dangerous Hong Kong becomes. Ron is attacked with knives and swords. He fights a dozen men at a time and his vengeance is so passionate that he cuts through them one by one until the assassin is revealed.

The murderer is his longtime friend and teacher of the 36 Chambers of the mind; the same mobster from Chinatown who sent him to Hong Kong to find out who killed Bruce. The mobster had planned to trap Ron in Hong Kong and kill him there without the American police to do an investigation. It was easy to dump a body in the river in Hong Kong in those days. People were killed every day in the city and dumped in the sea. Bodies washed up in the harbor and floated by the restaurants where tourists and people from the city ate nice meals. After Ron takes down the mob boss in Chinatown, peace is restored to the temple and the truth revealed to Bruce Lee's disciples.

He used all of his character to make it from each day to the next. He began to fight off stage because everybody was challenging him. The Asian stunt men were extremely proud of their skills in martial arts and more often than not he found himself at odds with them. Sometimes they came in twos and sometimes threes.

Ron was starting to make some big films while sowing the seeds of the Chinese Goju. Over the next decade, Ron wins nine more All American titles and four more World Championships. He continues to star in more Kung Fu movies acting as choreographer for The *Bamboo Trap* and *Black Dragon Fever, The Last Dragon* and *Way of the Black Dragon.* He stars in mainstream productions as well, cast in *Mule Bone* and *Roots;* where he was hanged and whipped to death in one scene.

Ron loved the Orient. No one spoke English and Ron had to learn Cantonese to survive, immersing himself in the culture. After several weeks he could understand what they were saying about him. The Chinese called him Hak Gwai, meaning black ghost. In Chinese culture everybody who is not Chinese is considered the walking dead and the Chinese people refer to those people as ghosts and by the color of their skin. Gwai Lo was the White Ghost. Ron liked their thinking and fell in love with the Chinese culture. Although he was a foreigner they made him feel at home. He lived in the barracks with the camera crew and learned all the components involved in the film making process.

There were a lot of good fighters in Hong Kong. A little fighter who weighed twenty pounds less than you might hit you upside the head with an open palm and drop you to the floor while you blacked out before you knew what hit you. Ron was never scared. The last people he'd been scared of were Smokey Stover and his father. Scared wasn't an option after boot camp and everything else he'd been through. He went so far out on the other side that if he didn't calm down, somebody would kill him. He had to fuck up jealous boyfriends so badly they made sure they didn't want to mess with him again. He was like Dr. Jekyll and Mr. Hyde with no control. He was over the edge like the wolf man. He developed a scary switch to turn off and on to deal with his emotions.

It wasn't very hard for him to kill a person and he was very good at it. He'd done his fair share of slitting the throat of the enemy. But he felt differently about it now. The war settled nothing. Executions didn't stop people from killing or stop the violence. The violence was an uprising of epidemic proportions. He knew it and disregarded the paranoia associated with it. He'd been shot at. He'd been beaten. He'd been stabbed and he'd been hanged now twice, both metaphorically and literally. His reality transcended the average paranoia. The Indians say that it's a good day to die and Ron had lived that philosophy since the day he was hanged the first time. The status of a superhero that he could not attain in the police force was achieved now as a movie star. He thought he could fly and went further out on the edges. Becoming a kung fu movie star was like being spun out on acid daily and they all actually were. And when they found themselves in opium dens in Hong Kong after weeks of debauchery, it was hard to leave a good thing.

His last year in the Philippines brought him fortune and fame. *The Black Dragon* played in movie theatres worldwide. He was a Kung Fu movie star in the Hong Kong action movie industry. They called him to sort out details for the sequel negotiating the terms for the script and choreography. His success in *The Black Dragon* surpassed industry expectations. There was going to be a new genre of martial arts' films in the Hong Kong industry and Ron Van Clief was the one tying it all together. He was their poster child; their black hero. He was a God in the Orient, respected and praised. He was on top of the world.

Chapter 18

Hong Kong Wing Tsun 1972

He woke to the sound of a horn somewhere down on the street echoing back and forth between the space of the buildings and into his brain. He was back in New York City. The sun was peeking through the towers shadowing the wall through his new venetian blinds. He walked to the window to look out over the city and stretch some life into him. He ran his fingertips along the bamboo and was proud that he'd put them up. They really added class to the place, he thought. He flipped the switch on the wall turning on the lamp. Everything was brand new; the couch, the television and the toaster oven. He smiled at his accomplishments and walked into the kitchen to make some coffee and think of ways to keep the money coming in.

Millie was still in bed with little Ron Jr. curled up next to her. Ron studied her gentle features from her eyes to her nose, her chin, then her neck and her tiny ears. Her hair flowed in reins of ebony across her shoulders over her breasts where her hand stirred when her sleeping mind sensed his stare. Ron was happy and this feeling warmed his stomach and his arms as he took a deep breath pulling in all the air to start the day.

He would start out on a run through the village to meet up with Zulu and spar at the Dojo. There was a joint in the ashtray that had been lit the night before but never puffed on enough to get it going. He'd fallen asleep, at what time he did not remember. He put the joint to his mouth flicking the Zippo from the table. Ron breathed in the smoke holding it in his lungs letting it work through his body into his fingers and toes. The sounds of New York began to play in his ear as he nodded through the blinds pointing out the movement identifying their composers.

The satisfaction lifted him in from the floor as he thought back on all the days since his hanging in North Carolina and his time in the war and everything after Pete's death. It was all there was for him. He owned it. His past brought him back to reality like clockwork ticking hands on the last bell of school for the day. He was free to go with all of his baggage to carry. Ron pondered these thoughts only long enough to accept them as his own; letting them go with the sounds in the early morning.

There was a knock at the door and he shrugged his shoulders as it was a peculiar time for anybody to be calling on the Van Cliefs. Through the keyhole he saw six armed men in combat-ready olive green and one Sergeant Major in his pressed blues. Ron inhaled another hit from the joint as he watched the men through the peephole, jumping back startled as the Sergeant Major pounded on the door with his fist this time.

"Lance Corporal Van Clief. This is Sargeant Major James Fitzgerald of the United States Marine Corp. Please open your door. We need to talk to you."

Millie woke at the second knock with Ron Jr. whimpering as she rose leaving him.

"Who is it?" she asked.

"Some asshole from the Marine Corp," Ron said scavenging any visible paraphernalia from the room.

"What does he want?"

"How the hell should I know? He's got half a dozen armed soldiers with him."

"Jesus," Millie said pulling on her sweater.

There was a loud smash as the door splintered off its hinges, hanging on an angle against the wall. The soldiers stormed in as if they were securing an LZ in the Tet Offense. They ransacked his house tossing everything on the floor.

"Mind telling me what all this is about, Sir," Ron said firmly holding his ground against the foreign intruders but paying respect to the three stripes on the Sergeant's arm.

"The American people need your services once again, Mr. Van Clief."

"The hell they do. I'm done." Fuck the corps.

He felt the butt of an M-16 hit his stomach knocking the wind out of him as he buckled to the floor. Millie struck out at the soldiers and as they wrapped her up submitting her, Ron was to his feet fighting them off. The blue suit Marine unholstered his pistol shoving it into Ron's face as they held him down on the floor.

"You're coming with us dead or alive. The choice is yours."

The soldiers escorted him out of the apartment and down the stairs to the street to several vans.

"Where are we going?" he asked.

"Classified information," snapped the Sergeant Major. "Have you forgotten your level of classification?"

The vans pulled into a tall building with dark windows in the downtown area.

"Why not use a blindfold?" he asked

"It doesn't matter. You're a Marine," he replied. "Releasing classified information would be treasonous and you'll be hanged."

"Been there, done that," Ron said and the Sergeant smirked an unfriendly grimace across his mouth.

The soldiers escorted him through the lobby to the elevator where two of them broke off securing their posts. He was led to a small conference room on the 9th floor. Six men sat around the table with their papers in front of them. Two of them had brass. One was Army. The other was from the Corps. A guy with a white collared shirt sat next to a scientist with glasses formulating charts and probabilities. A man with a black suit and Italian silk dress shirt opened to the breast, sat back in a chair with his relaxed fist up to his lips stroking the slope between his chin while whispering to a British man with five o'clock shadow and suspenders smoking a cigarette.

"That will be all Sergeant."

The Sergeant stood at attention saluting, turned and left. The man in the suspenders leaned in on the table.

"What have you been doing for the last five years, Mr. Van Clief? You became a police officer fighting crime and made yourself a movie in the Philippines. Becoming quite the action star aren't we."

"It's just life after war," he said arrogantly. "They told me I needed to move on from Nam."

"Except it hasn't been much of a life now, has it Ron? Men tried to kill you. They hanged you. They tried to kill you and you didn't die. You withstood all of that and tell me son, how did you do that? Please forgive our urgency. I trust the men who brought you here were cordial."

"We got along swimmingly," Ron mimicked, waiting for the sugar coated part of the interrogation.

"Tragically," said the man in the black suit with the slicked back hair now gesturing with his hand. "We live in a world where evil men wish to harm innocent people."

"Is that Vietnam you're referring to? That nice little stroll in the park; where we kept the children safe on their swing sets and merry-go-rounds?"

"The war is over. Times change."

"Sorry sir, I didn't take you as the Bob Dylan type."

"It's a tragedy what's happening in our country today, I'll agree with you, but mind your surroundings and the company you're in now. You aren't so far removed from rank that we'll have you reinstated on the next assignment to Northwest Alaska." The man in suspenders grew irritated. "The point is," he redirected, "the enemy adapts. We're fighting a new kind of terrorist. Their entire plan is to bring down Western civilization like the Communists and the Nazi party wished to take over during World War II."

"So what the fuck does this got to do with me?"

The brass-clad Marine came out of his chair smacking the table with the open palm of his hand.

"I don't know what the hell kind of shit you've been smoking or where you get your drugs from, but you better get your shit together. You're a Goddamn Marine so act like it."

The Army man clasped his hands together taking the time to let his words build the platform they were pitching. Ron had no choice. They blackmailed him with his son. The special investigations unit of the CIA was conducting an interrogation at the military base in Guantanamo Bay. Somehow Ron's qualifications and profile fit the criteria and he left Millie and Ron Jr. and went to Cuba for three months kicking the shit out of 100's of detainees. In order to maximize the terrifying effect of waterboarding, the interrogators conducted mass waterboardings with twenty people at a time screaming and drowning, begging for mercy and squealing the information floating in them. They attached battery cables to men's genitals and force fed them super laxatives to keep them dehydrated and miserable. But they paid Ron well and after three months he was allowed to go back to New York City where he and Millie would raise Ron Jr. The money was good and Ron continued his acting career, diving in head on.

Ron had everything he wanted, but the reintroduction of war into his life tormented him back into survival mode with nobody to fight but himself. He went into a deep depression and assumed all responsibility for Pete's death, attempting suicide more than once, sitting back in his room with a bottle of Jack and sleeping pills. His grief was suppressed by the mind bending drugs at the VA hospital. His mind was numb. The only thing holding him from the edge completely was martial arts.

There were only short moments of happiness when he could bond with his son, but the filming on the road took its toll on his marriage with Millie and in 1978, because of the partying, Millie left and became a United States Marine.

Millie left Ron and their child. Ron was down, but not out. With no money left, he begins writing *The Manual of the Martial Arts* and its first printing became a best seller on the New York Times Best Seller List, picked up by the Secret Service and introduced as a defense training manual. Ron sells a hundred thousand copies. The commercial support for his martial arts encourages him to become a Grand Master Red Belt. Ron surrenders everything else to raise Ron Jr. and pursues the dream of a Grand Master.

Chapter 19

Frank Ruiz, Peter Urban and George Cofield

Ron had built dojos all over New York City. He was training three hundred people a week between the school system and private lessons. Overnight, Chinese Goju became a popular thing to do in America. The public loved it and the Asian film industry promoted it. Ron starred as the hero and together with other big name experts, helped set the standard for what martial arts is today.

There had to be a way to tone it down. The sport was violent. There were too many broken bones and knocked out teeth. Guys were drooling on themselves after three fights; repeated concussions and permanent brain damage. Guys were killing each other in the streets for money to put bread on the table. They got better at it. In Asia, Ron was tested. A black man on the street is a phenomenon in China, and also is the obvious outburst of his presence among a shorter race of people. He was enormous. His hair made him stand higher; puffed out and groovy, big choppy sideburns pointing down. He moved like

Jimi Hendrix played the guitar; from another universe. The streets were a matrix filled with villains and gangsters who wanted to test their styles of karate on the Black Dragon. The true kung fu masters sent their disciples out on missions to find the best fighters to bring back so they could fight them themselves. Martial arts is a lifestyle. There wasn't a person in China who didn't know at least some form or discipline. The motions and the practice lined out a profile for everyday living. Ron Jr. grew up as a black Chinese. He didn't know the difference. At the age of three he could already do spinning head kicks. His first language was Cantonese. He grew in his first years under the traditional influences of Chinese culture. But Ron was afraid to deprive his son of the America he loved so much. He didn't want his son to grow up without English speaking friends; without ever seeing another black child his own age with whom he could identify. He thought about New York City, but it brought back dangerous memories.

In New York, Ron taught many famous people and became a bodyguard for a number of famous actors. One of his students in Chinese Goju was Danny Guida. Danny Guida was the son of the Vice President of Ghana under the Akuffo regime. In 1976, Chief of Defense Staff General Akuffo and other members of the SMC, seeing the low esteem into which the military was using the public's discontent for General Acheampong's misrule, staged a palace coup on July 5, 1978 to remove Acheampong and accused him of running a 'one man show'. The coup maker formed SMC 11 and made Akuffo Chairman.

Danny gives him the perfect opportunity to escape the concrete jungles of American subculture again and Ron goes to Africa on the ticket and pay of the Akuffo regime, riding the coattails of corruption. He took Ron Jr. He'd taken Ron Jr. all over the Orient and Ron Jr. was a rock star. The Asian girls loved him. Ron Jr. had spent more time in the Orient actually than he had in America. Now that he was getting to be five or six, he thought he was Chinese. After Millie was gone, New

York left a bad taste in both of their mouths. Ron took his son to the motherland to find their roots.

When they first got to Ghana, Ron was assigned a female agent: an automatic, card carrying, steel hard, supermodel, bitch packing juice. One call and shit was happening. She was Ron's girl. She did everything Ron wanted. Ron started working for the military in Ghana and the Ivory Coast. He had a thousand students in Ghana alone. He trained soldiers and the police and government troops for both countries. Ron became a hero again and felt he was truly at home for the first time in his life. There was no end of money. He had everything he and Ron Jr. needed. He had dozens of women taking care of them daily and because he was friends with Danny, he was always chauffeured around in a bullet proof limousine.

Danny was a bad seed. He had diplomatic immunity. He would take briefcases with three or four pounds of coke through customs because the customs officials couldn't do anything when they found it. Danny was so bold he would just throw eight keys of coke through the security machine without so much as a thought. DEA got fed up and Danny lost his privileges to come back to America. The Akuffo regime was filled with people like Danny. The regime initiated moves to return the country to civilian rule by instituting a new Constitution Drafting Committee. General Akuffo lifted the ban on politics but banned 105 prominent politicians. Despite his efforts at returning the country to constitutional rule, Akuffo did not seem to have the answer to the country's economic problems as workers who could not make ends meet, took to the streets. The Akuffo regime was a typical despotic government, raping and pillaging all of its own resources and natural wealth. The people were starving and their leaders ran around fat and happy.

On May 15, 1979, less than five weeks before constitutional elections were to be held, a group of junior officers led by Jerry John Rawlings attempted another coup, this time against the Akuffo regime. Initially unsuccessful, the coup leaders were jailed and held for court martial. On June 4, however, sympathetic military officers overthrew the Akuffo regime and released Rawlings and his cohorts from prison fourteen days before the scheduled election. Although the Akuffo pledged to return political power to civilian hands and addressed the concerns of those who wanted civilian government, the young officers who had staged the June 4th coup insisted that issues critical to the image of the army and important for the stability of national politics had been ignored.

Unlike the initial period before General Akuffo where rehabilitation effort focused on the powerful elite, this second attempt at reconstruction from a situation of disintegration was propelled by growing alienation. It strove by reforming the guidelines of public behavior, to define anew the state power structure and to revise its inherent social obligations.

In retrospect the most irreversible outcome of this phase was the systematic eradication of the pre-Akuffo leadership. Their executions signaled not only the termination of the already fallacious myth of the nonviolence of Ghanaian politics, but more to the point, the deadly serious determination of the new government to wipe the political slate clean. Rawlings and the young officers formed the Armed Forces Revolutionary Council (AFRC). The armed forces were purged of senior officers accused of corrupting the image of the military. In carrying out its goal however, the AFRC was caught between two groups with conflicting interests. These included the 'soldier-supporters of the AFRC' who were happy to lash out at all manifestations of the old regimes; and the now organized political parties who decried the undue violence and advocated change with restraint.

Ron had a good friend who was a newspaper reporter who disappeared right after the coup. He was too vocal about the government. People disappeared and nobody said anything. Everybody knew, but nobody talked. Danny fled the country in the middle of the night on his father's private DC10. Ron was alone and didn't even know it. Danny moved to Ireland and his father moved to Switzerland with $300 hundred million they had stolen from the government. Ron was friends with a government official and now he was a nobody and alone in the country. They started killing and making people disappear the day after Danny left. That was the day they confiscated Ron's car and house and everything else he owned. Troops came to his house and put a gun to his head to make him leave. The troops took Ron and Ron Jr.'s passports, telling Ron's bodyguard to take him to the airport.

On the way, they were stopped at a roadblock. When the officers came for Ron, they put him on his knees in execution style. He pressed Ron Jr. to his chest and closed his eyes. The officers spoke with Ron's bodyguard as some of his captors slapped him upside the head while he was in handcuffs. Ron Jr. is what saved him and the fact that most of the guards recognized Ron from their training. They wouldn't kill their sensei. Ron left Africa. He saw Danny a decade later and tried to play it off like they were cool. He ended up giving Ron a large check.

Chapter 20

They travelled around the world riding the wave. In the end, when they could find no solid grounding and the money he made in movies was spent, Ron took his son back to America and in America, the drugs found him once again.

Ron put his money together with three veterans who were drug dealers and bought a government building from habitat for humanity on the Lower East Side of Brooklyn. Ron tried again to build a home for his son, but they were surrounded by drugs. The building was being used by the other veterans as an operations center for junkies all over the city and they were always trying to get him high. They didn't care if the building was ever finished because they dealt drugs. Ron owned the first and second floor. Each guy had his own two apartments and built them up themselves or had somebody else do it.

They owned something from all the work they did and Ron made it work. But eventually the other vets didn't want him there because he interfered with their business. Ron was teaching martial arts classes to kids in the backyard all the time while inside, there was heavy traffic. Ron was left without a choice, so he left. He and Ron Jr. were homeless and moved into an abandoned building four blocks away. They had no refrigerator and no running water. There was no electricity.

Doris stepped in and helped Ron to raise Ron Jr. and also helped to deal with Ron's state of mind. The culture shock in addition to the drugs and psychotropics was once again too much to handle. He was no longer a superhero. He'd lost his flare. Ron Jr. walked into his father's bedroom to ask for help on his homework on a school night. Ron had a gun in his mouth and was about to kill himself. Ron Jr. remained quiet in the shadows in the hallway peeking through the sliver of light between the door and the devil's house which held his father. He knocked on the door softly and went in.

Ron broke down and reached out again to the Veteran's psychiatrists and reintroduced himself to the scene. He underwent hours of electroshock therapy to deal with his PTSD, insomnia and nightmares. In 1984, still broken on the inside of charisma from the shadows, Ron is inducted into the All American Hall of Fame at Madison Square Garden. His achievements as a 15 time All American are acknowledged.

He started doing films again with the Screen Actors Guild and finds extra work in the second Batman movie with Val Kilmer. Ron was Val's bodyguard. Val was brilliant. He had a super high I.Q. and became a great swordsman martial artist. He was a chess player, had a sword collection and he had humility. He was so talented. Val could read through his pages on the way to the set and speak his lines in front of the camera like a tape recorder was coming from his brain and he said it like he meant it. It wasn't mechanical. Brando couldn't remember his lines. He had to use idiot cards his whole life. In the movie, *On the Waterfront*, when he's talking to his brother Mickey, what the audience sees is take 80 or 90 because Brando was so cooked. Val was dedicated to his life and career and though Ron was his senior, he found himself under the study of men like Val who could focus their minds without drugs.

Inspired, Ron travels again to the Far East seeking truth through martial arts and meditation. He goes inside the realm of schizophrenia to chase the dragon. He returns to America again and writes four more books. Networking and promoting himself, Ron continues to build his reputation amongst celebrities and because of his background in the Marine Corp and martial arts, becomes the instructor for the United States Secret Service.

IIis life was backwards. He still clung to his friends and clients like Richard Pryor, George Benson, Eddie Murphy and Wesley Snipes. Ron had built himself up again on a mountain of clouds. He had everything he wanted but it felt unreal. He was still suicidal and restless within. He was incapable of having a healthy relationship with a woman. He gets married and divorced five times and has two bastard children. It is all he can do to keep from running up the ladder of intravenous intoxication and jumping off the Empire State building. The realm of the psycho paranormal is unforgiving. The only rite of passage is to fly through the gates of incomprehension. Ron stumbles on the metaphorical trail of the mythical beast and hunts down the dragon inside of him to take wing above a life so microscopic, no pulse of individuality remains. The time would be remembered to the rest of society as the 90's.

Ron never gives up, hunting the beast relentlessly, putting himself under the microscope threatening to multiply. Ron enters therapy and begins to tear down walls. Dr. Killebrew, the vet therapist, makes him come face to face with the past. Ron is dissected and starts falling apart inside over the lessons he is learning. How could he pull the trigger on all those people? He was just following orders. Vulnerability develops you until you're like a mountain that's invincible. Hoping for a comeback, Ron goes for the last win or loss of his career and enters Ultimate Fighting Championship #4 at the age of 51. He fights Royce Gracie and loses by a rear naked choke. As he fought the choke against Royce, he goes to sleep. When he wakes up, he is still fighting the choke. He becomes the Commissioner of the UFC and helps build the organization to what it is today, on the verge of becoming a high school sport.

Chapter 21

**Ron Van Clief and his brother Conan Lee at the Hong Kong
Freefighting Championship**

Until two months ago, I didn't even know who Ron Van
Clief was. In all the research I find posted about him, I see an
unconditional respect for what seems to be an iconic figure.
My curiosity for martial arts never grew beyond doing my own
voice overs for my friends when we watched drunken boxing
and the Wu Tang Clan. For all intents and purposes, I'm a lost
writer trying to find his way in a world at war with words.

"So let me get this straight," I say, licking the glue through
the paper, following up an easy line from the filter to the end of
the cone, tapping it tall and twisting it, shaking it, then rolling
it again between my hands like a Cuban as I had learned in
Amsterdam from the Moroccan immigrants. I flick alight my
Bic to roast the end and inhale the mid grade I picked up from
the Rasta outside the convenience store at Koki beach. I'm
exhausted. Ron made me fight the whole class at MMA tonight
to teach me something I haven't figured out yet; to teach me
how to get my ass kicked and get back up again and walk

away. I can't move except to twist the spliff. "You're like a Ninja right?"

"Over the past fifty years, I've probably done all the major forms of martial combat starting with Jiu Jitsu." Ron hits the spliff. "I learned from Peter Urban. He was the best. When I met guys like Sensei Ruiz, Kemfoia Padu, Sekwii Sha and guys like Rick Pascetta, I got my ass kicked. What you did tonight was nothing. These guys are pathetic."

"I had to drop my black belt at the Urban School in Chinatown when I first started because guys were kicking my ass. Sensei Urban brought the Japanese style of Jiu Jitsu back to America from Japan after he studied with the Grand Master Yamaguchi. Ruiz started Nisei Goju. It means second generation. Sensei Ruiz decided that he wanted to do his own style and he got the authorization from Sensei Urban. He started developing Nisei Goju which pretty much ruled the tournament circuit from the 70's to the 80's. We were superior; like 300 hundred Spartans and every week we would travel to a tournament somewhere in the region."

"Tell me about the animal style."

"There are twelve animals? Or are there 36 animals? You hear about the twelve or the eight or the sixteen. But there are thirty six because of the 36 chambers of knowledge known by the Chinese. The basics in the Chinese martial arts systems are based upon animals they should never have seen. There were no lions in China. The Chinese only knew about the animals because they travelled the world and did research. They were way ahead of the rest of the world, especially in combative arts. China has been invaded by every country in the world and they are still China.

"Sensei Urban made me fall in love with martial arts more than anybody else. He had what nobody else had. He had control over his head and spirit. He would play Chopin during class then knock some student's teeth out for being disrespectful on the mat. That was the kind of man Urban was. One day two cops came in with their shoes on the mat. He kicked both of them in the stomach, disarmed them and threw their guns in the elevator shaft. He didn't care who they were. They had stepped on his mat. The mat is a field of respect.

"Urban studied with Mas Oyama. Oyama was built like a refrigerator. He created a style called Kyokusinkai which produced the toughest style of karate fighters in the world. Oyama liked to wrestle with bulls. The scene was glorified by Sonny Chiba in the movies when Sonny captures a young bull on the rampage and chops him in the top of the skull then finishes the beast by ripping off its horn."

"People really did that?" I asked. "What kind of drugs were you on? I mean, were you stoned the entire time? Who kills bulls with karate chops, seriously? What happened to paranoia?"

"There was no paranoia. I never got paranoid until I started bouncing at the Electric Circus. While everybody was tweaking their minds out I was cool as a cucumber." He passes the spliff back over. It burns slow as I rolled it with a perfect pull as loose as it needs to be. "I don't remember competing straight," he says exhaling his last hit. "Man, I studied the animals of the Chinese system. I emulated the dragon because of its mystical and mythological omnipotence. There were different colored dragons that have different skills. That was me man. I would go through color periods like Picasso."

"And now you're the dragon!"

"I'm the Black Dragon."

"Are you high?"

"A little."

"It's not the best."

"Hey man. This is great." And then asks me, "Have you ever done heroin?"

"No."

"Heroin is really strong. You don't have to do it long to want to do it. It's the most relaxing hit. It's like an opiate hit when everything is floating. The whole thing is very amazing. You walk real slowly while trying to compose yourself. It's out there. Sensei Urban could tell when I was high. He would just tell me to GI up. He didn't care what we did as long as when you were on the floor you were the Black Dragon or whoever else you were supposed to be at that time. He appreciated creativity and different outlooks on life representing one's own journey within. Sensei Urban idolized President Theodore Roosevelt for instance; his swagger and demeanor and he gave him credit for bringing the first martial arts to America. Roosevelt brought guys in from the Orient to teach him Jiu Jitsu. Urban liked the diversity."

"Would you like some tea?" asked Simina from the kitchen. She saw right through him.

They met in the 90's in New York. Ron was working at Radu's midtown 57th street. It was *the* health spa for diplomats and celebrities. He would train ten to twelve clients a week in martial arts and fitness. Most of them were high profile like J-Lo, Matthew Broderick, Cindy Crawford, George Benson, Bianca Jagger and Mick's whole crew. Radu and Ron met during karate class with Frank Ruiz.

Radu had defected from Romania during the period when Nadia Comaneci who after the show at Madison Square Garden, drove to the United Nations and declared diplomatic immunity. As well as having a way with the ladies, Radu was very talented in multiple sports; the decathlon, archery, skiing and biking. He'd attended the same sports institute in Romania where Simina would later go. When he opened his gym he wanted trainers from Romania. The wall came down and Simina was brought to the United States.

"Do you remember the wall?"

"It was just a game of control; a political game with all the worst intentions of master manipulation. The wall only came down for distraction. The powers that be were just doing P.R. work. Open up places like Romania or wherever and then two years later they're wondering why everybody is doing drugs and listening to rap music. They get it from television and they create their own demise. You can't expect it to be any different. That's all we give them. We sell it all over the world. We're not in a race war today. We're still in a power war and that's all it's ever been; power to move vast sums of money to control what happens. Nothing can be changed from individual effort. Those people are at such a level that if they even think you might impede them they will have you killed. The guys in international security did things like looking in on us with satellites. They have every kind of surveillance equipment you can think of. It's like in the movie, *Enemy of the State*. These people have their own satellites and thanks to the Clinton administration, so does every other country in the world."

"We could be shot for talking about it."

"We don't matter."

"We are like Shakespeare to make a mockery of our society."

"They let us get away with it and then they pay us."

"Peanuts they pay us. Let me ask you, what's the cost of slavery?"

"Thank you for the tea."

The door opens and closes. A child is screaming. Words are spoken between a man and a woman. The door opens and closes. Ron sits down again.

"He's so beautiful," I comment.

"Women…You know women can't really handle men children; little boys.

"That's one of the problems with children out of wedlock. Women are trying to raise boys on their own. There's no structure. There's no male figure to knock you back in line."

"I think she objects. When she comes home he doesn't pay any attention to her. When I come home it's like Daddy's home. You know it's a big deal. But she shouldn't have resentment over that because I was around all of his life in the beginning and it's just as if I was the dad who was out working and she had the better relationship."

"The roles will reverse as Kai gets older. There's going to be a time when he doesn't want to talk to you at all."

"She says she's having a hard time handling it now. I told her to wait a couple years and see how she likes it then."

"It's her first child?"

"This is my fourth." Ron stated.

"I hear you didn't raise your voice."

"I never do at least I try not to."

"What's the point?" I agreed.

"It doesn't settle anything. It makes them more stressed. And we can't help them that way. A woman has built in mechanisms that have nothing to do with us men. Leave them alone if you don't know how to use the gear. You follow me? Their system is hardwired into the main frame of humanity. When I was younger I had no patience at all for women. I wanted sex or money. I didn't care what a woman said. I had my agenda and that was that. So imagine," he said as if imagining showed a perspective to any other man today worth his salt. "We're going big time. I mean really big. We're going to be on all the talk shows."

"Let's do Rosie."

"Let's do Oprah."

"Let's do Wendy and Ellen; all of them."

"It will be a manifestation of two men's imaginations."

"It's not a dream, my brother. This is reality. Please, you are my brother now, Sparky." Ron said. "You take the place of him now that he is dead."

"Then that's it. It took us this many thousands of years to get back together; *White Snake and the Black Dragon*; a dynamic duo of super capers. You know, I like it. Suit and tie. Spit game in the minds of the ultra-saturated cesspool of tabloid gossip. We will sell one million copies of the book in the first printing. What do you think?"

"Absolutely! Of course, absolutely."

"The roller coaster of freedom transcends the darkness of confinement."

"You haven't seen anything yet. Wait till it's finished. It's going to be ridiculous. Ridiculous I tell you. I can't tell you how ridiculous our life is going to be. There are ten publishers right now waiting for the manuscript as we speak. It's a game. You give me enough pages to make it worth somebody else's time to read and I'll make sure we don't have to worry about money for the next five years. Write it down and send it off to Tarantino, Lee, Singleton and the RZA. Make it a blockbuster.

"Call it, *Night of the Living Legend: White Snake and Black Dragon*. America needs more superstars. We cannot live in the past and pretend to be dead people. The culture is ready for a way out. The people want to believe in real life exploitation between theirs and the movie stars. You are Shidoshi, Grand Master Red Belt 15-time All American, 5-time World Champion and 250 pushups in three minutes. Ron Van Clief aka the Black Dragon. We will show the world why you are who you are. The reason people will support the Black Dragon is because of your spirit. When you said to me that one man cannot change the world, I agreed with you, one man cannot change the world. But we are two men and our army is thousands upon millions and their army is millions upon billions and that's how one gets things done if one wants to infiltrate the psyche of the public mass. You've done it already. We are the mythical creatures who turn the sky in the night time. If we don't steer our world, our stars will fade away and burn out in the darkness."

"There's no other way," the Black Dragon said sadly. "This is the final stand. All the years of practice and discipline lead up to the final moment."

"Until the next final moment," I say.

"Shift the whole focus to then, when and if that time ever comes. Once you overcome the darkness and overcome the fear of having a gun in your mouth, every second is a slip into death and that's where you have to live forever."

"Every day is right now and we're not going to give a fuck. Did I say it right?"

"You got it."

"Should we find something so precious just to let go of it?"

"I've paid my dues. I just want to do the work and be the father."

"What's the hardest obstacle you've had to overcome?" I asked.

"My brother Pete being killed in Vietnam," Ron says. "I'd just left there. I should have been killed. And then Danny goes and gets killed. How fucked up is that? I never got over that. That part of life is dark for me. It will always be dark. Pete was a year younger than me and I know he had a baby girl just before I got out of the service. I've never met her and it makes me sad."

"Do you dream about him?"

"I have for years."

"What do you dream? What do you see?"

"I just see us as kids, playing."

"He's never come to you as an older person?" I asked.

"He came to me as you. We had a hard life in Brooklyn. Imagine Jose's girlfriend jumped out of the fourth story kitchen window while we're having dinner one night. Come on man. You know? He couldn't go in the service because he had a bad criminal record and he was a real tough guy. He was a very special guy. He was a genius, but he went totally to crack. He would leave his inspector's shield for the department of sanitation with the drug dealers as collateral for crack until he could come back with enough money to retrieve his shit. Kirk was the same. He used to be young and neat. Now he's completely fucked up on dialysis on a machine that he carries around eve-rywhere he goes every single day of his life."

"What's opium like?"

"Oh man," Ron smiles into a distant memory.

"Does that make you happy thinking about it?"

"Yes, I have been lost a long time on opium waiting for my friends to come and get me out. 'You've been here for four days' they'd say when they'd find me."

"When you were making movies?"

"That's right."

"I'd be there right now, you hear me, if it wasn't for those guys and as long as the royalties kept paying in. Imagine. It was ridiculous. You're tripping and you see three chicks down there. What's happening? It's nirvana man."

"You were a very svelte young man. All the girls were in love with you. You were the big shit. We saw your films. My girl was in love. You were confident. You were bullet proof."

"I'm still a baby, understand? We're all delicate. We sur-vive only as long as we can. As I get older my body starts getting delicate too. I can't push it like I used to. What a drag, you know?"

"You got to keep up with the science. You have decades of foundation. I told you I feel like I'm 20 again and that's due to the discipline in the martial arts world."

"Isn't that crazy?"

"Jiu Jitsu. Tell me, what is different about New York and Urban's style than say Okinawa and Japan?"

"Compared to the Philippines or Korea for that matter? The difference is when I started in the 50's, fighting was purely for self-defense. There were no tournaments. There were no mixed martial arts at that time. There were only guys who returned from the service who learned martial arts in Korea. They brought back Jiu Jitsu, Judo and Karate. There was a lot of input that way. We started developing our own style from what we could get a hold of. I learned how to box from my father. I fell in love watching the old boxing matches on television. We took boxing, submission and striking and developed it into a sport here in America. Today's MMA was used for self-defense in everyday life in Asia for ages. When I was there, everybody wanted to fight me; even extras in the movies I was working on."

"And in the street fights?"

"Everywhere! Hong Kong movie stars tried to fight me because I was making movies on their turf. They didn't like it when I came around the corner and tuned them in Mandarin. Go screw your mother you bunch of monkeys. I'll take on all ten of you sons of street trash. You are the little one they call the rat, Aren't you? I was tripping through all of it. You have to know who's got the better stuff out there. You have to seek it out and find out who's better than you so you can beat them. By the hundreds I would take them on if they came at me. Do you understand?"

"Yes, Shidoshi."

"I've been stomped. I've been beaten. I've been everything. I've dealt with all of it."

"And you survive."

"You have to. Do you want to die? You get up and get the hell out of there. Life is crazy. I went to Vietnam. I am a Marine. I killed people with my bare hands. That is who I was trained to be. I am an assassin. When I was hanging out with Bruce Lee…I believed all of it. This is life and this is who I was born to be. I'd been lifting weights when I was eleven; getting pumped up, brain fucked up by society on who I was supposed to be. I would run into twenty guys in Hong Kong. I would attack them. I would murder them. 'Your mothers eat dog tongue for breakfast', I'd say…take another hit of opium…and let my mind wander to the end of the universe and let the universe take over. I lost everything."

Chapter 22

Aiki Snake with Jamie Milnes

The night is filled with the chirping from Koki frogs in the grass beneath the palm trees scattered out along the beach. A cool breeze blows and a wild rhythm beats inside both of us. We are survivors. We are warriors. We wander the earth in search of the truth and reality in all misunderstandings; look as far as the stars can go and then disappear into the focus of the darkness of a black hole among us; stepping outside of the inside, out of everything; to walk into the jungle with countless eyes shining down upon us somewhere beyond the fray.

"I'm in a scene. I'm the choreographer. This guy's coming at me harder and harder. I'm taking it because I don't want to mess things up. I want to kill him. There is some sort of friction. Turns out I beat down his little brother in the neighborhood. On lunch break the guy says to me, 'Do you want to spar?' He was just some fucking Chinese stunt guy. You know a young punk, so I took him in the back of the building and I gave him the beating of his life. I put him into the side of a garbage can and stomped the heel of my boot into his forehead. I didn't fire him. I didn't tell anybody. It was one of those kinds of beatings. The director saw it and nodded. It was beautiful.

"My Kung Fu teacher Leung Ting at the time was the one who got me into the serious ideology of Wing Chung: an angular, straight line technique of blocking and countering at the same time. It involves fast hand movements; a lot of trapping and working on basic movements on the vitals; eyeballs, throat, balls, the efficient vitals only. Probably Wing Chung is the most practiced systems of Kung Fu in the Chinese system. There are a lot of variations of Wing Chung, but the basic premise is the block and counter. Bruce Lee didn't originate these ideas. These were principles that existed in the Wing Chung system three hundred years before he made them famous. The Wing Chung system was created by a woman named Wing Chung. The advancements in the Chinese civilization allowed for women to develop art forms such like that. Wing Chung was using her style three hundred years before now."

Kai runs in and tackles me.

"I want to see."

"Do you know what this is?"

"I want to see."

I show him my black hole device. "It captures all of the present and escapes when I take it through the other side. Your father and I are discussing very important matters."

"I want to talk," Kai insisted.

"Don't worry. We record everything you say, always. They've been recording us for a long time. Everything everywhere is captured somehow somewhere. They have access to everything and can use it against you when they want to. Say something. Say anything."

"My daddy loves me."

The span of a daydream fills the silence and we're brought back from way out there.

"I've been through hell," Ron says. "And this is my reward. I have a baby boy after all of that. Right now is the happiest time in my life. You're so special," he says to Kai, grabbing his son up in his arms.

"We can never do everything we want to do, but when I fought the best at sixty, I was beating them easy. 'Is this all you got?' I had to ask. Is this all the world can give me, having suffered what one man must live through in a life? It's a real big deal when you become a world champion once, but twice, three times, four, five; a lot changes. I'm invincible at five World Championship titles. At my age, I have to wonder what they're building these days.

"It's horrible. I teach fourteen and fifteen year olds who can't do twenty pushups without falling over. In four schools there isn't one. I lay into them. They are so weak and pathetic, engorged with junk food like they have a welfare credit at the Kentucky Fried Chicken. I have a running bet at all the schools, $50 to any kid who can beat me doing pushups. I've had four of them try already. One did almost 80. I did 150 and then I stopped because I didn't want to make him feel bad, only to show him where he needs to put his mind. Do you understand me? I say, 'I'm an old man; gray hair, almost 70 and beating your ass. Just do fifty'.

"That's why I feel now that those kinds of things are getting to me and I'm feeling old because that's what it is, the difference between people now and then. People are not tough like they used to be. People are not hardened for the blows that are coming. Our society builds weaker men afraid of the dark. My body gets older. The machine breaks down; the organs, the blood vessels, my nerves."

"What's the worst…drugs?"

"Martial arts…doing drugs for long period of time has an effect on you; decades of blow; the years in the service shooting up; the 60's *and* acid? Yah, it has an effect on me for sure, on my brain, but I just feel lucky to be alive. I could be a homeless junkie in New York City or dead."

Beneath a skin tight t-shirt are vascular clubs of a coiling leopard, relaxed and deadly, ready to end a man's life faster than a mamba's bite.

"My body doesn't make me money anymore. Ideas make us money. Get me words and I'll send them to the editors. Let them do what they got to do so we get a movie deal. You're nothing without Hollywood. This is my story. Write it."

"Thanks, I guess? Take it and do what?"

"Do what you will. Spill it all over; mercenaries of space, separated by the dawns of time reflected in the sapphire waters of the Virgin Islands; the story of a lethal weapon."

"Doctor it up a bit."

"You're out of your mind. If you want me to doctor this thing up, give me a couple years or salary. I don't have time to think about writing, old man. Write the whole story in two months? Have you gone mad? Of course…I know you are tired already in your young life and already you think you have done enough."

"We won't fail."

"Neither one of us will sell ourselves short. I know it's a rush, but once we publish, we'll be huge. Overnight me the manuscript the minute it's finished."

"Just make it happen?"

"Do we have a choice?"

"We chose this."

"Do you think my first book was finished? They turned it into a text book and it became a best seller. Don't give up. Never quit!"

Kai whimpers. "Daddy, I don't want to be a little boy anymore."

"What do you want to be, a chicken?"

"No."

"A dragon?"

"No, I want to be just like you. "

"Oh, I love you man. I want to be just like you."

Kai is a baby ninja. He jumps from the trees and stairs and the roofs of houses. He is just a frog.

"Give me that foot."

"You'll never take my foot, Daddy."

"You're a bully, Frogman. Take this you little brat."

"No. I don't like it, Daddy," Kai says as he stabs a plastic toy screwdriver into the Black Dragon's neck.

"You're a donkey," says the Black Dragon.

Kai stabs him again.

"This ends the peace between us. Of course you know I cannot surrender and let you walk away. I will eat your eyeballs or your belly first and then your ears, you donkey."

"I don't like you anymore, Daddy."

"I don't care because Spiderman loves me."

"Spiderman loves me Daddy, and he doesn't love you."

"Aquaman loves me, Frogman and he doesn't love you. Let's ask him. Aquaman, do you like Kai?"

"Kai is a chicken." said Aquaman.

"You're a chicken, Aquaman."

"Spiderman says I'm not a chicken. Spiderman likes me," said the Black Dragon.

"Quiet," screams the frogman and stops. "Daddy, Let's talk."

"What do you want to talk about?"

Kai screams and jumps over the Black Dragon and strangles the beast by the neck with his amphibian legs. The Black Dragon shrieks out roaring fire. Time and space were frozen slowly on the event horizon one last time as Kai held the Black

Dragon by the back of the head and the toy screwdriver to its neck until…

"We must be free, Sensei."

"You're right. There is more work to do."

"We can make a difference in the kingdom of beautiful sunshine?"

"One more shot so we don't have to hit the punch card ever again." Kai punches the Black Dragon in the nose.

"We're done. No more toys."

"You're not my daddy."

"What did you say?"

"I apologize," Kai said.

"Not good enough. I told you not to do it before."

"I apologize. I apologize."

"It doesn't matter."

"I apologize!" Kai screams. In the seconds of impatience the world is ending. The sky is falling down and the oceans are rising to the drowning terror of teardrops caught by the cheek of a bristling wind.

The Black Dragon laughs. "Send it to Spike Lee, Quentin Tarantino, John Singleton and Clint Eastwood"

"Daddy, say I can do it."

"You can't do it, Kai. You can't do anything because you are a piggy."

Kai laughs.

"Who's my little ninja?" Ron asks bending over to give his son a hug.

Kai punches the Black Dragon in the nose again and the Black Dragon eats Kai my action hero.

Chapter 23

The Black Samurai

America is an evolving society which must adapt and do everything possible to ensure its survival. The country had been overtaken with its own technology created from its own worst nightmare. America gave up the goods and sold out but they gave everything away first and made a mockery of the people.

It was the fall of the Roman Empire; a country on the first fringe of that downward spiral. It was an irreversible cycle. People get fat, lazy and brain dead. They've bought it and started copping out of it the second they tried to sell it. It was time to look for a new planet to live on because everyone here on earth had fallen asleep. Something died inside of people, took their spirit and went away.

It happened in the 80's; kids with bleached blonde hair, the dawn of the Citation and the spawn of the Eagle. The guys carrying washed out condoms in their wallet because recycling was the cool thing to do. The boundaries had all been broken down and the secrets all unlocked. Show to the world that we won't hide who we were or what we've done to become who we are. Minds were under the influence of such terrifying substances. It was during the filming of *The Last Dragon*.

"Explain it to me. You were coming off of this high from being a movie star making so much money and all of a sudden you just lost it?"

"I lost everything several times in my life."

"Why? The women, the drugs... Nam, being hanged? At what point did you start to lose everything?"

"I was living in New York with my fifth wife. I came home one day and she was having sex with her ex-boyfriend. I walked out with just what I was wearing. You can lose everything at one time like that. I've had a couple of those. It's all good though."

"Did you always know you were going to be ok?"

"You just keep going. Adversity builds character. Take the opportunity and don't look back. Life is not a negative. See it as a new path and never look at the past with regret or you'll hate yourself for it. As long as you're above ground, you're alive. When we regret there is trouble. We ask, 'what is this bullshit again and why me?' And this and that and how did it all and who could have, what if it was or it wasn't? Keep moving. That is what defines our generation up until now. We're still moving but we're shit and it's pitiful as we disgrace the heroes and minds which precede us."

"You're disappointed in your generation?" I asked.

"Yes, I would say I am disappointed with my generation. We used to have a damn good generation and we let it go. We had brilliant minds."

"Are you done? You speak of it like it was over."

"We did have it, but now there are only remnants of it. We have good remnants from it, but a lot of people fell down and only a few stayed up doing their thing. It was living the life and surviving. It was the good life though. The good life probably took those others down and the ones who got up from that are messed up forever. Everything that could be done, I've done," Ron said staring at me. "You hear me? Everything! LSD goes nowhere in the end so if you feel strong enough and try it just for the experience one time then stop, you'll be ok. But if you keep doing it you'll end in complete ruination. Total fucked ruination; financially, physically, morally and in whatever other way.

"There was a man from New Orleans who slept on a sofa his entire life and he loved LSD. He was a crazy squatter who paid no rent. He took two buildings from the city and sold them. He lived in no man's land for twenty years and paid no rent for twenty years. He is still a photographer. He took a building from the city because the people who owned it lost the building. It was the city's buildings and people moved in to fix them up. They paid no rent.

"Buildings like that were all over the city. There was a collapse in New York in the late 70's and people needed a place to live. They were just shells broken apart and torn up. It was a bad time for a lot of people. Everybody moved out of New York. They couldn't stand it. The businesses moved out because of taxes. Everybody talked about leaving and they did. The city was a ghost town. There were no more tax dollars. It was filthy and nasty.

"This man was very creative in how he lived. He never worked but always had a scheme. He was actually selling apartments from the city to people moving in when it was supposed to be free to live there. He lived there for thirty years rent free and charged everybody else rent. There was sheet rock hanging from the ceiling. You could see up two floors through the floor joists and there was nothing covering them. He never cleaned. Clothes were stacked in piles. His place was a maze.

"Kwame was a tripper. There was shit everywhere; sculptures, a pile of clothes hangers, plastic bottles. More stuff for one of his projects he was working on all the time. He had two floors. The first floor was a war zone. On the top floor he had his studio. That was immaculate. Everything was spotless. You can't have dust if you're a photographer. The bottom floor where he lived was really bad and because there was no electricity he'd run the ovens and the gas all the time. They had tapped into the city's gas and then eventually the electric lines. They did everything. We're talking about twenty apartments more than half of which were filled with crack heads and drug addicts. There were maybe 10% who really wanted to do something. Everybody else was just there for the free rent. It was a big space and free rent. He lived his dream.

"I did all the work in that building," Ron said. "I was one of those gung ho mother fuckers who mopped the whole building from top to bottom. I would do it weekly. I would spit shine and gloss the banister on the stairs all the way up to the sixth floor so you could see your face in it. I painted the whole building myself three times; the entire thing without the other owner's help because none of those fuckers gave a shit. My son helped me and some of my students helped me. Guys were tapping into my electricity through the walls. For years I didn't know. They went through the walls and spliced the wires. These guys were technically pretty smart. Imagine living in a building for thirty years without paying rent. Imagine living in

New York City without paying rent on the Lower East Side. Millions of people made their dreams come true," Ron said.

"I wanted the challenge to do this. I felt like a homesteader. I was in it deep. I fixed both of my floors and cleaned up the whole building. I did that for seven or eight years but nobody was interested. Now I live in the islands in the sun.

"My point is that I just was amazed at how strong this guy was to live this way and be happy. He enjoyed himself all the time. He had plenty of pussy and he was always stoned. The guy was a good photographer. He had all sorts of movies stars. He was a true bohemian. I got him a SAG job shooting photos but he didn't care. He did really well but he'd come one day and flake off for a few weeks. He was so nonchalant. He was on every welfare program there was. He milked the system. He played the system like the insurance scammers today. He was unbelievable then. But I stopped doing the homesteader thing and went back into film."

"With all the trauma the world must bear, we are alive looking out at the islands and darkened periods of time and can come to realize the enlightened situation. Now that we're here Shidoshi, how do we inspire the rest of the people?"

"Talk to them. Everybody stopped talking to each other. They're texting on their cell phones. Everybody just stopped talking when we used to only talk before. Before there was technology to distract us people had to find things to do. You had to have friends and people and talk and connect. It's disconnected today when they think it's really connected. The circle's been cut in half and tilted off of its axis. We have to connect.

"When was the last time you went out of your way to do something nice for a random stranger? That's where you start. Everybody is always judging and calculating each other's next move. Who can we trust? We are the mirrors of one another.

We are the reflection of all we see. We can't trust ourselves because I know what you do because I would do that also. The assumption is made that you will act in a certain way. The feelings come; the emotions and the anxiety and we haven't even taken one step. Then we're popping pills again that are no better for us than the street drugs we get so we never get off the drugs and the whole cycle goes around again.

"In the book *Huckleberry Finn*, Huck and Nigger Jim are floating down the river on the raft and they get to the town with the snake oil salesman selling potions and elixirs. That's what you and I are going to do to them, my brother. We're going to tar and feather all of them. The next time we meet we'll have our own television show. The point is that it never changes. Here were two fellows masking the truth of what they're really selling. They marketed elixirs with extraordinary claims and people bought it. It's a cycle. It plays over and over until it becomes its own religion. You have to write because there is nowhere else to go," Ron said.

"Do you think the man on the side of the river who's been looking at fish his entire life, who has never moved from that one spot under the tree, cares what people think about how handsome he is? He thinks about how handsome the fish are and the people passing by know that he is thinking the fish are handsome so they think that he is a handsome fellow even though he might not be. It's not because of his face or anything else but because of his spirit. When you can see the lines on your face you can see a kind man who has gone through suffering and you wear this pain and suffering on your arm every day for the rest of the world to see. That's when the biggest test comes and perhaps the best results."

So much had changed, I thought. The places we've come from and the tomorrows we reach for. The feeling of entrapment comes to mind when you sum up the illusions of paradise in one sentence of 'fun in the sun'. Inside, my heart was on fire. My brain was on full drive still half asleep from the time I spent idle before Van Clief. Go as hard as you can when you're doing something. Why not? Why wouldn't a person go as hard as they can and do everything in one fail swoop move onto the other and do it all over again. How many of us are super heroes? How many of us have the capabilities? I won't say it isn't everybody in some way, but who definitely is, must step out into the world from amongst us. It was a heavy burden to carry.

I drove around St. Thomas in the night remembering some friends I had to catch up with just down the road at a pub by the water for some dancing and drinks. When one thinks of the Virgin Islands they must think of paradise. I'd lived here for a year now without the complete satisfaction of the stereotype. The island was a mess. The hills went up and down and nothing ran on time. The American territory had barely stepped beyond third world mentality only to hold it together with the hip hop culture again. The direction the world was going didn't surprise me and I have to admit I shut it off. It had been over a year since I'd sat down to watch the news. Newspapers were a waste of time because they all said the same thing and never told you the truth. After all, the life of mine was the one I would create if I had a choice. Sometimes we don't have choices and I viewed my situation as one who treads water. I let the vodka and energy wicked up my system for a few more words in my vocabulary and said goodbye to the faces for the summer. Everybody would be leaving soon to go north. I would starve it out through the hurricanes. Or would I? The timeline for the book was more ridiculous and the more words I put together, the more it tied itself into a living asylum.

Chapter 24

One could never know the past of a man without being that man day in and day out and the only thing we can ever do is tell a story. Was the book a masterpiece? Of course it was. I didn't have a doubt. When you doubt you die. That's how it was presented to me and I believed enough of what I'd already seen for myself in life. I would chase the dream that can't be caught to the ends of the earth because I believed so strongly in catching it, I would pull the trigger with the barrel in my mouth if I abandoned or neglected my own talents.

The pages came as they did in their own form. I didn't have to think about them. Time was time enough, by myself in my own head and not in the bottom of that stinking war vessel with the heat smothering me. Everything smothered me now. The leaches sucked at my appendages and my neck. The island pace would drag me down if I let it, but I could not. I was stronger than that. If Ron could do it than I could do it if he thought I could. If he thought I could do it and I didn't then that made him a liar and I wouldn't ever call him that. We dissected his brain digging up while watching a basketball game or on the floor of the living room. His heart suppressed so much hatred. There was so much he never showed the world of his pain and suffering and eventually even superheroes lose their strength to carry on.

We could only beat each other now. And because I knew I wouldn't beat him I gave him everything I could so that when he left I'd know how to beat the rest of it. Tonight I would beat myself up a little bit and I didn't care. Something so misunderstood that the common place ideal could not comprehend such an elaborate scheme. Only the truth could reveal such a mysterious epiphany. On and on it goes. As my mind spins around I'm only drawn to one place where I center myself in the beginning of the galaxy and the world of this place; the beginning of time, the creation of life and the spawn of civilization. Broken down into pieces to be kicked around walking down the street at night; terrorized by the shadows of the same illusions we elude ourselves with right now in this period of time. How can one know? One cannot know the sequences and vibrations of the molecular structure of the universe unless he knows it's engrained inside of his genetic pattern and subconscious. Tear it apart and build it back up with the elements of our own substance. A quibbling mad man we say not, for what else do we have to live for today if we cannot reach that one goal which is communication? That is the hardest and most destructive thing we've ever had to do. For with the communication and unification comes the opposite; demise of the civilization scorned at each other. The sequence hounds in squalor. What should be done about the masses? What should be done about the justice? I plead the case but the case is never different. It's always about the same thing because I know you and you know me and we cannot fool each other lest we fool ourselves and are forever in that deeper burden of a flaming portal of our alter egos to be changed on that infinite timeline.

All there is left to do is speak and I'm speechless. I've surrendered the body. I've surrendered the soul. The passersbys come in shadows. They do not know that they do not see. They are lost in their dream world of hypnotic fantasy, controlled by

the modernist technologies we have created from our psycho-
fanatic perversions for pleasure unbalanced against harmony.
Beat me down with clubs. Stab me with knives. Poison me.
You cannot sleep on the park bench my fellows. Only the
awake are welcome. If you're not present then don't present
yourself. Forget what's been stolen from me. I did have to walk
the dark street until the lights came on again and I found myself in the afternoon. There was a light of gray as I walked
down the boulevards trying to find my way, contemplating another scheme that we could actually shrink the space that's
wasted in our minds and fill it with the wisdom and knowledge
we all yearn for.

The wheel is working. The package is in the hands of the
most influential celebrities in the business. Because Ron is
great they will help sort through the madness of a bottled up
writer and get this thing right. He can't wait. The Oprah Show
left a message. I was at the beach and asked to not be disturbed
by anyone except Meagan Fox. We're going to Hollywood and
there isn't time for additional distractions. Tell her to take a
seat on the beach and have a lemonade.

"We are on the road and life passes by," Ron says. "I know
we are one more step closer to catching the dragon", Ron continued. "So why am I so disappointed in people? I'm mad at
myself for investing so much in them in the first place. It's
happened a thousand times before in the race against time.
We're on the road now and they expect us to turn into something. We're going to turn it in and we're going to get paid for
our minds.

"Who else can we talk to? I can't talk to 90% of the people
around me. When can you find a real person to talk with who is
special? That's the reason they're there because their minds are
going. They're pulling us out of the worm maze inside the matrix.

"They're looking for projects. They are looking for ideas. They've got people looking for guys like you and me. I'm going to make a deal with one of these fuckers. They're going to have somebody write the screen play. We're going to be home free. We're going to be consultants on our own fuckin' movie just chilling. Get ready to do the press junket. That's what's up. I just ordered myself a nice blue Gucci Tuxedo. I'm ready; eight hundred bucks. We can't go on Oprah looking like hippies.

"You can do what you want to do when you're in the game, but we're coming back from the dead. They expect me to be wearing the same tuxedo they buried me in. On a whole other level it's not the same. Hopefully nobody will recognize us.

"We are on the road now. We might not even see it yet, but we're on the road and the minute you finish the writing, the moment you give me the pages, it's going out to the screen writers. Once we sell this it's going to be over."

"And build a multi media empire?" I asked.

"Wherever we're going from here is limitless. To me it's just another book and another movie. Nothing special. For you, it's about taking advantage of all that's in L.A. And you know what's crazy? Now that we've gotten to this point I don't know what else to write about but I do know what we should be doing; how we should live life. We're always talking about how one lived life instead of how one lives life. It's beyond the scope because everyday ideas come and go and are gone. They become old ideas in the matter of seconds. Every time you can think about is gone. There is only the present time. The Now! When we where kids we never wrote anything down When we were children we used different words and slang to express ourselves and then we developed with our environment. We used words like rad, awesome, cool and then gnarly and now gangsta. It's always changing from when you were younger. It was our own language that came with its own hierarchy of when the words could be used."

"Are you comfortable with where we're going with this?" I asked. "Are you comfortable with how we're proceeding? If you have any suggestions or questions, please let me know because I want to be on the same page."

"We have an open door policy between us. When we're on the talk shows and you have something to say, don't hesitate. You must say what you have to say."

It had to be maddening in my own mind. There was only one way and nowhere else to go, deeper inside the mind of the Black Dragon. He assured me it's what they were looking for. It would be nice to get a couple million for a multi-book adventure and a miniseries. When you take people from life out of the woodwork and put them in the spotlight their star begins to shine.

"I want to go away and chill out," he told me. "I want to put you on the road with these fuckers. I don't want to do anymore acting. I'm tired. I don't want to study scripts. I don't want to read dialogue. I don't want to memorize shit. Just get this book finished and we'll make a movie out of it and chill the fuck out and feel assured that you are in the right place to mess with all of these fuckers out there. We're going to push as hard as we can on this. All we need are more pages. Tarantino will be the first one to see the finished thing no matter how finished it is. We'll send a copy to my list of top forty. Then book tours, talk shows, a press junket, upfront looks. Both you and I could use an extra few hundred thousand dollars. That would be a good way for you to start out your life with a nice chunk of change in your pockets. You'll also write with the best people in the business. I want to finish this project so these people know who you are and that you're capable of writing whatever project they put you on, period. If they know that then you'll be working for more years on this deal."

"Then, there is only one question left to ask. What do they want?"

"They want style and content," he replied. "They will package it and send it out to every book house around the world. Your job is done. When you finish it, they'll pass it over to two of the best screenwriters they can find."

"At this point I just have to surrender."

"I know how it works man. I know what they're looking for. I like your style and I like your energy. They will like it. It's totally commercial. That's all we're looking for on this. You're going to be writing other stuff. Start working on screenplays. That's going to make you more money than writing novels. Believe me. That's where the money is. You write one great screenplay and Hollywood will suck you up like a vacuum; you'll be tired of writing before you know it because they'll drain every bit of creative juice you have out of you. That's what Hollywood does when they find a talent like you. You hear me? You take advantage of it and make as much fucking money as you possibly can. Got me? The day you finish the three hundred pages or whatever it is you're going to do; you and I are going to sign it, copyright it, then send it to the Writer's Guild. That will be your first credit; you've got one project in the Writer's Guild.

"And it goes on from there, I thought, building up cities in Detroit. Building back the country and taking the world from this sandstorm. It's a mess. It's all confusion and nobody can make sense of our world today.

"Decide what you're going to write next. It goes simultaneously with everything else. You can't fight the urge to write when it's building up inside of you. People always talk about life instead of living it. I've done all that shit. I'm done with it. Roll one for the road and we'll smoke it."

"Yes sir."

"Do you see that it's totally feasible? We send it off to these guys and you and I jump on a plane to California and do it. Would you like me to get an extra ticket for your lady friend?"

"Um, I guess so."

"We'll see what Hollywood has to offer. I'm psyched. I'm more than ready. I'm psyched. "

"I can't do what I'm doing every day, going back to the beginning again. I feel so disappointed because I see so much compromise in people's spirit."

"You're going to see that forever. You better get used to that," Ron declared.

"How do you not be dragged down by it?"

"You won't. I won't allow that. Not as long as I know you and I'm going to know you until I die. You hear me? You helped me do my life's story. You are a part of me and don't realize that yet. We're like Siamese fucking twins right now."

"Do you mind if we smoke this spliff here?" I asked.

"Go right ahead."

"Siamese fucking twins."

"That's the way I feel. In the deepest darkest jungles in a cave in Africa, somewhere in Ghana a man woke up screaming. Ten years from now you'll call me from Hollywood and tell me you wrote this screenplay for this movie that's been nominated for an Academy award and you've been nominated for the Best Screenwriter. I'll be there to see you get that award because you have that potential. You can do it. You don't see that yet."

"I feel it."

"I know it."

"I know that it's there."

"That's all it takes."

"We'll just knock it out in a couple of months and be done with it; end of story."

"Lights out."

"I wish I could stop time."

"There have been times in my life that I wished I could stop time," Ron said thoughtfully. "I almost got killed in Vietnam because I was so into what was happening. I was out of ammunition still holding the trigger down. Think about that for a second; belt finished, empty. I was so scared that I would end up in a body bag. I would do anything not be in a body bag. That's the terror you can never release from your body. It's at the base of my spine right now."

"Do you fear that the situation will return?"

"I hope that nobody ever pushes me to the point where I have to kill them. There's no thought. It would be easy. That's my fear. My wife knows I have a temper. I don't want to deal with people on that kind of level anymore."

"You're so gentle."

"I don't know if I could control myself if somebody raped my wife. I would kill them. I would rip off their head and shit down their neck. It would be the other Ron. I said that for years and my shrinks thought I was schizophrenic for a while. It was so painful to think of what I did that I referred to myself in the third person to not be that. I can't think of 1965 without going through some kind of psychodrama."

"Yet, it becomes casual."

"You know what my wife says all the time? That was so many years ago. Why don't you just get over it? She does this to me all the time with all of this hyper-vigilance I have behind me. How can I expect her to understand it? She's never seen anything terrible like that. She's never seen somebody murdered in an ultraviolent scene. How can she identify to people seeing that shit done to them every single day; people you know, people you don't know getting loaded up on the trucks in body bags? You thought we were joking? You can't joke. Even if you get away from it, you still know that it's happening. When new guys are arriving with new supplies and the trucks all the time you know what's happening. We're losing people in the field and these are the replacements. Even when I went to Vietnam they were loading body bags on the boat. It was a real wake up call. I knew it was coming, but wow. It was like Rambo in real life with people getting their arms blown off in front of you. How long do you think you have to see things like that before your feelings change and you have no respect for human life; not even a roach? I never thought about any of the things I did until I got out of the service years later. I never thought of what I did as anything. So what? I shot people from a helicopter. That was my job. They gave orders and that was it.

"The things veterans have seen make them suffer all of their lives. I know plenty of guys who attend these reunions. Guys from K Company who I served with are there. When I see these guys in wheelchairs and some of them with their faces blown off, I see the real tragedies. It's comforting to see them because no matter what kind of shit they've been through they're here. They've beaten war. We left 57,000 dead bodies in Vietnam. I go to these meetings and see two hundred tough mother fuckers. These are the guys that don't take care of themselves. They've got beer bellies and are fat. They're done." Ron continued, "They're toast, but what a spirit for survival. I had five wives before I married Simina and thirty some odd shrinks. None of that ever got through to me. Everybody was like that. I'll ask a guy where he went and which place he went into and if he remembered any of those people.

"I was there in '65 and they were doing the same exact shit in '69; bombing mother fuckers and killing gooks, going back in for a day or so to get pussy.

"I just wanted to take a piss. I could feel my teeth floating. I'd been waiting all day for it. Met a marine from camp LeJeune in special ops who couldn't tell me what he did. He could only tell me what he was capable of if shit ever happened again. I stepped into the bathroom. There was a drug deal going down but that doesn't have much to do with me. I'm just trying to get to the next level; trying to keep ahead of all the people trying to steal my ideas. I can't put it down on paper fast enough before they take it away from me again. I saw a goat in the parking lot and it made me think I might prefer a goat to a dog as a pet. They're just as smart and they have horns. Dogs don't have horns.

"What really concerns me however, is how it all goes down. Life isn't any different than it's ever been. Man just becomes aware to more of the situation; pornography, drugs and corruption. It's all been there since the beginning. Man can only be initiated when he reaches a certain level. Even the best guy asked how I deal with working my ass off fourteen hours a day at a job I don't like. I can't forget about it. It's in the past and that's where it will stay.

"What happened?" Ron asked. "We're going to think about losing each other again. We're going to think about the time when we must separate from each other rather than the time we have together. You can change the scenery but it doesn't change the situation for any of us. We can't just go to New York City and become rich overnight. That's the Hollywood dream; I'm going to go become a movie star; I'm going to be rich and famous. You can't say that because everybody says that. We are already movie stars with God watching. There's a spotlight on us all the time. Whatever character you want to play is who you're going to be. We just keep auditioning over and over for different parts. Evil lurks around every corner. Look for the spirits in the darkness and hear the crickets on an African morning and the hyenas cackle on the outskirts of ram-shackle patches of tin. And I was so disappointed in a woman. Not that I felt betrayed by her for the sake of loving me but for her lack of wisdom and the decisions she made; because today there are so many beautiful women going after substandard men and they don't care about the warriors in the best of them. They only went for the pockets. You have to hold on to her as tight as you can because she is so beautiful. She can't be re-placed. One wants to know what love is so you'll take her and squeeze out every bit of love from her because one day she will go away again and you'll call me and we'll cry together. That is life. Enjoy it while it lasts. How can we think we can hold onto something forever when we can't even get inside our own minds for a second? The Rasta on the side of the road will spend the rest of his life there picking through the trash talking to the fleas on his shoulder.

"I almost left out the best parts," Ron said with a surprised tone. "You have to love her because she is the best part of life. If I cannot love a woman right now with the time that I have then when am I going to love and who will I give it to? I'll have to give it to somebody. If I have nobody then what am I doing? We're like the customers who talk themselves out of the sale. They come into the store with the intention to buy and then end up talking themselves out of it. I know when some-body will buy. It's all about finding out where they're from and where they're coming from. Once you know that and you've opened it to trust, people will buy anything you're selling. You have to close the opportunity. The people who are in front of you are not by coincidence. We have to find the reason. Maybe we share the same birthday. Maybe we have the same color eyes or have been to the same national park once in our life and we can share a vision of what we saw once upon a time. For those few seconds we share, we recreate the moments of happiness that are ours together again forever. Nothing can take that away. You'll spend money as fast as you can to keep those memories with you just a little longer. So often we overlook the people in front of us because we've already decided where we're going to go or what we need to be. You have to find your time."

Chapter 25

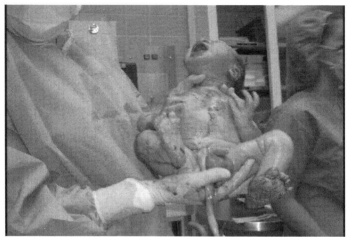

Kai Van Clief taking his first breaths

IN RON'S OWN WORDS

March 13, 2006. 07:38 a.m. I, Ron Van Clief watch Kai take his first breath with the umbilical cord hanging. The doctor holds Kai by the back of his neck while I take a picture with my digital camera. I must have looked like an alien to him with the face mask and gloves. I held him for a moment. I was truly overwhelmed by the experience.

In the bathroom behind the delivery room I passed out onto the floor after looking at the digital still. Big tough marine, fainting like a girl at the sight of Kai covered in blood. I actually had a bump on the side of my head from hitting the bathroom floor. When I became conscious the digital camera was laying next to me with Kai's picture displayed. I picked up my camera and washed off my face and hands. Simina and Kai were lying in a hospital bed. Simina looked like an angel. Kai was beaming. He knew mommy and daddy. The nurse gave me a towel, mask and gloves so that I could hold Kai. I put him on my chest, sat in a chair and fell asleep with Kai on my chest holding him.

Simina and I had arrived at the hospital the night before. Imagine having a child and becoming a parent again at 64 years old. It was one of the most wonderful experiences of my entire life. Exhaustion set in and Simina told me to go home and rest. In the taxi I kept looking at the picture of Kai. Kai being born has given me another 25 years of life. Because I didn't have a loving and caring father I tried my best to always show unconditional love to my children. My wife thinks that I spoil Kai, but look at it my way; my time with Kai is limited and I want him to be happy. His smile makes my heart shine. When he says you're the best daddy in the whole world...it literally brings tears to my eyes.

As I aged and grew my feelings became more sensitive. Kai and I cried at the end of the movie *Real Steel,* a story about the relationship between father and son. Trust and love were the foundations of the movie. We actually went to see the movie again. Beautifully, our eyes were a little teary at the end. The love and pride the son felt for his lost, then found father was emotional to say the least.

I want to live long enough to see Kai graduate college and get married. To see his children is the optimum plan. Kai is six and I don't know where the time has gone. It is true that when you age time goes by quickly. I figure in 20 years transplanting organs and limbs will be status quo. The cure for all the diseases that we now know will be available. So I only have to make it another 20 years to get the rebuild. During the now time I will work out every day of my life and prepare for the future. While at Lyons VA Hospital I learned one coping skill that has been useful to me on many occasions: pause and breathe.

Chapter 26

The Black Dragon's Revenge

IN RON'S OWN WORDS

For over thirty years I worked in the film industry as an extra, photo double, stuntman, stunt coordinator, action director, screenwriter and director. Some of my performances stand out in my mind! One such experience was on the set of *Homicide,* the long running cable TV series. It is in reruns all over the globe. This episode was about the murder of a white man whipped and hanged in Harlem. The murderer was an African American descendant of a slave killed in the 1860's in the south. The slave, my character, was Zeyphus Rigby. The murdered victim was found whipped and bound hanging from the ceiling. The background story of my character was he was a free man who was captured by the KKK and turned into a slave. He was whipped, beaten and hanged. I was hired to be a stuntman but landed the part. It included several scenes as a slave in the fields. One scene was the slave owners chasing five slaves in the high grass at night under the moon. It was so cold I was shivering. We wore almost nothing except for coveralls and ragged shirts. It was a surreal experience.

I had the chance to feel the fear and anticipation of the scene. Even though I knew it was just a show, my body still felt a level of shock. Several of the stage hands made jokes that I found offensive; professionalism and self pride guided me through the ordeal.

In the last scene I was being shackled and dragged into a barn. There I was whipped to death by a female KKK member. She was known for taking free blacks and selling them as slaves in the south. As I look back at the situation, I knew why the other black stuntmen didn't want to do the extra scene. In those days it was just a job to keep Ron Jr. and myself eating regularly. I never really enjoyed the film industry. You met some very talented actors and actresses on the set, very few of which would ever remember you if they see you again. Stuntmen and women make the actors look great. We save them the bumps and bruises as professionals.

Chapter 27

IN RON'S OWN WORDS

In the 1970's in Hong Kong, stuntmen worked extremely hard making kung fu stars look tremendous. Accidents happened all the time. Jason Pai Piao kicked me in the temple on the set of *The Black Dragon*. It almost knocked me out. Working on Hong Kong films is an adventure. My first Hong Kong film experience was on the set of *The Black Dragon* shot in 1973 and released worldwide in 1974. During my seven week shoot we were on location in the Philippines and Hong Kong. It was my first time appearing as a principle/star of a feature film.

Yangtze Films had signed me up for a five film contract. Contract player really means slave. I was paid $500 per week plus hotel and food. I would have done it for nothing! It was my dream to become a kung fu movie star.

I learned how to speak Cantonese by necessity. First you hear them say the same words day after day. The words have meanings that you sense. It is amazing I was able to converse a month later in Cantonese. I learned lots of Tagalog during the shoot as well. My co-star Jason Pai Piao was a veteran kung fu movie star with over 50 movies under his belt when I met him. I learned a lot by watching his performances on and off the set. He had attitude. I taught him several spinning and jumping kicks for his fight scenes. He taught me the basics of martial arts choreography and screen presence. Jason was a good fighter on and off the set. The film was a real low budget shoot. That is just the way movie making was done during the 1960's and 1970's. It was a wonder experience as I slept in a dormitory/barracks with the camera crew and production team. We worked as a team. Jason didn't know I was a fan of his work. Watching him on the screen made me want to become a kung fu movie star. He was dynamic and charismatic. All the fight scenes were shot out of order and I never knew what scene I was doing because there were always changes in locations and personnel.

The whole film was shot in seven weeks. Edited and in the local movie theatre in another month. I enjoyed every day on the set because of the professional yet very friendly team spirit. The crew was hard working, capable and worked like clockwork.

The days were long, 10 to 12 hours a day was very common. Sometimes they pushed the limit of human exhaustion. We would move into a location and be ready to shoot within an hour. The director Tommy Loo Chun was a veteran of Shaw Brothers studio as a stuntman and director. A nice guy who spoke not a word of English but was great with sign language. I really respected his work as I had seen many of his films. The bad guy was Thompson Kao Kong, another kung fu film veteran with over 100 films under his belt. Between Jason and Thompson I gained much of the cinematic attitude and presence I have today. Screen fighting is a total art unto itself. Chinese and Japanese fight directors are the best in the world.

I was totally exhausted by the time we finished shooting *The Black Dragon*. I had no idea it would become a blockbuster in global release. The immediate star status was overwhelming. I didn't know how to cope with autograph hunters and the far too numerous fight challenges in my future.

On the set of my second film, *The Death of Bruce Lee* aka *The Black Dragon's Revenge,* a stuntman challenged me to a fight on the set. When I finished the scene I was shooting, I faced his challenge. Some of the other cast members including co-star Charles 'The Pantera' Bonet watched as we squared off. Charlie was the first Puerto Rican kung fu movie star. The stuntman was a very good kicker without any close quarter defense. When he attacked, I moved in and hit him with a rapid punch combination and swept his legs from under him with a dragon tail sweep. He fell backwards onto his head. As his back hit the cement I lightly stepped on his forehead with a stomp kick. I helped him up and we laughed it off. The crew and cast cheered in the background.

Most people that see me in the movies thought it was a stuntman or camera tricks that made me look good. I had studied the martial arts for over 17 years when I got the opportunity to become a Hong Kong movie star. I was the first American to headline Hong Kong Kung Fu movies. Mr. Serifim Karalexis and Mr. Yeo Ban Yee were the producers of *The Black Dragon, The Death Of Bruce Lee, Way of the Black Dragon, Black Dragon Fever* and *Super Weapon. Super Weapon* was the first martial arts documentary to be released worldwide as a theatrical feature film.

My friend and mentor Grandmaster Leo Fong hired me to star in the action film, *Bamboo Trap* totally shot in the Philippines in 1974. It was supposed to take four weeks and turned into two months. Leo was a very good director and studied with Bruce Lee. He was a strong man with excellent boxing skills, as well as a Baptist minister with a great left hook. He almost knocked me out in a hotel room on the set of *Bamboo Trap*. Leo produced, starred and directed the film. Darnell Garcia, a world karate champion was cast as the bad guy. Of course I kill him at the end of the movie. One day he and I were sparring in the hotel room and I got a busted lip and Darnell received a black eye from the action. Leo was really upset with us. After that we just worked as hard as possible to finish the film. Lots of rain and bad weather added days and weeks onto the shoot time schedule.

Bruce Lee had opened my eyes to the wing chun style of kung fu. Bruce referred me to Grandmaster Leung Ting. Leung Ting was a closed door student of Yip Man the founder of the wing tsun style. Leung Ting and Carter Wong opened up the doors of Hong Kung martial arts hierarchy to me.

I made a few friends and started teaching them in Manila. Every weekend I had off I would go to train with my students. We would go to all the different kali and arnis schools in the Manila area. Escrima and silat were blade and stick arts originated in the Philippines.

I met Grandmaster Remy Presas and received personal training from him for the complete length of the shoot. Shortly after, I invited him to New York for Modern Arnis seminars held at Sensei Peter Urban's School. He was a wonderful man and great teacher. If there is a big dojo in the sky GM Peter Urban, GM Moses Powell, GM Remy Presas, GM Frank Ruiz, GM Ronald Taganashi, GM Ed Parker and GM Bruce Lee will be doing their thing. Personally I don't believe in the hereafter. I believe in the here and now!

Chapter 28

Bushido

IN RON'S OWN WORDS

In the late 1960's I was the victim of one of the most bizarre events in my life. At the time I was living on 10th street in a 6th floor walkup. I was working as a transit police officer at the time and spending most of my time at the karate school. One day I worked a late 8pm to 4am tour. When I returned home I discovered that someone had entered my apartment and trashed it. Everything I owned was cut up with scissors and knives: clothes, food, shoes, karate uniforms, towels, pictures, books, magazines and trophies. My pictures with Bruce Lee and Chuck Norris and many others were torn apart into little pieces. I sat down and looked around at the mess. I didn't know what to do. Eventually I threw everything away in the garbage.

Strangely enough my next door neighbor was the culprit. Three days before this incident my neighbor was beating up his wife. I heard her screams and knocked on their door. He answered the door enraged. He tried to kick me in the balls. Of course I gave him a beating...just a couple of punches to wake him up to reality. As I turned to leave he took a hatchet and chopped at my head. I side stepped and the hatchet was lodged in the frame of the door from the powerful swing. I kicked him in the stomach and he fell backwards into his apartment. He was unconscious when he hit the floor. The police came and she did not want to press charges for his abuse. The police took him away. That was the last time that I ever saw either one of them. After that I always minded my business! Life is so strange. Anything can happen at any time. Can you imagine losing everything that you own in one day? From this experience I learned not to value possessions.

Chapter 29

Ron Van Clief wins All American Karate
Championship at 60 years young

IN RON'S OWN WORDS

By the time I reached sixty years old I thought my life was over. The year was 2002 and I decided to fight in the All American Karate Championship. The promoter Mr. Cho sent me a poster for the event. Immediately, I got a magic marker and wrote RON VAN CLIEF 1ST PLACE WINNER. Three weeks later, I again challenged myself to competition. My three opponents all much younger and much taller than I was, had their chance to make their reputations. In over 50 years of competition I never trained for one specific opponent, I just trained as hard as I could to get in the best shape possible. Everyday I would work on the heavy bag and speed bag. I lost ten pounds which increased my speed.

No sparring whatsoever was necessary to ready myself for the All American. My friends, Rick Aidekman, Ross Kaye and Howard Niego accompanied me to Queens College for the event. My wife Simina recommended contact lenses for sparring. It made all the difference in the world. How retarded we men can be at times. I saw what they where doing before they did it. It was truly amazing. My eyes acted like sighting devices and my arms and legs did what they were trained to do for five decades.

My first opponent was a 30 year old tae known do black belt with superior speed. His problem was that he was a typical competitor - fast in and out for the points. He didn't expect me to be so aggressive and attack first. As I attacked I grabbed his forearm to keep him controlled. Then I delivered multiple kicking and punching mechanisms. I won the match even though the opponent scored the first two points in a three point match. Enough was enough. I scored the next three points and won the match.

My second opponent was a moo duk kwan black belt about 35 years of age. At six feet four inches, he never scored one point although he tried very hard. I shut him out with three points in a row.

My third opponent was an old friend and dojo brother from Sensei Urban's school. He would be my hardest fight of the day. He was six feet five inches at about 260lbs. A David and Goliath match. He scored the first point with a face punch. I was trying to set him up for a combination but he was a smart tournament fighter. He was playing chess and not leaving any openings. I decided to give him some targets. I intentionally dropped my guard so that he would attack my head. As he punched towards my face, I blocked and counted with multiple punches and kicks simultaneously. The score was one to one. My next combination forced him to bring his arms up to protect his face. He never saw the round kick to his rib cage. It knocked all the air out of him. Actually he never recovered. My third point was a hand trapping maneuver that I learned from the wing chun system of kung fu. The rapid sunfist punches to his face were too quick for him to react or defend.

The match was over. It was truly an amazing day. My student Taimak borrowed my sparring gear and placed second in the middleweight division. I gave the trophies - 1st place sparring and 1st place kata to my friend, Hector Martinez. It was a good day! The Black Dragon and the Last Dragon competing at the All American Championship in 2002.

Chapter 30

Kung Fu at RFK Theater – *The Black Dragon*

IN RON'S OWN WORDS

An important part of black martial arts history is the All American Championship. The All American Championship celebrated its 25th anniversary in 1988. Taimak 'The Last Dragon' and I went to Madison Square Garden to compete in kata, weapons and fighting. The winter of 1988 was brutally cold, so Taimak and I took a taxi from my lower eastside homestead apartment. During this period my son, Ronald and I lived in a homestead on 7th Street. For a quarter of a century, the tournament was held at the Madison Square Garden's Felt Forum. In 25 years of competing in the All American, I placed 1st fifteen times.

Traditionally it had been a tae kwon do tournament, but as the years rolled by many different stylists competed. Kung fu, karate, silat, hapkido and many other hybrid styles were seen.

It was the number one tournament in the United States promoted by Master S. Henry Cho. It was common knowledge that you have to be five times better than your opponent to win.

To fight at the All American was a decision I had made one week before the event. In those days I was always tournament ready. I was bored and wondered if I could take first place at 47 years old. You question whether your machine can crank up the required repetitions. It was time for a reality check for myself. The first event was kata. Kata is shadowboxing like a boxer against imaginary opponents. I never considered myself a good kata performer like Louis Delgado, Errol Bennet or Chaka Zulu. Kata was too predesigned to feel comfortable to me. They were indeed performers at the highest level. There were many excellent kata performers in attendance that day. That day I did Sepai, the favorite form of my teacher Grandmaster Peter Urban.

Black belt kata is the highlight of the pre-fight competition. Four judges sit in a row in front and signal to begin by bowing and naming your style. All the good guys were in competition that year - Delgado, Miyazaki and Oliver. The cream of the crop. I knew it would be hard to make it to the finals. During the execution of kata, you are so focused that you don't even see the crowd of people around you. The warrior mind! It is you and your technique flowing together as one entity.

That day I was really psyched up for the event. Taimak and Ron Jr. kept me souped up. They were my own cheering team and I consider Taimak a son. The judges computed my score and it was a tie for first place. I had to do another form to break the tie. The form I selected was the Phoenix because it had a variety of flying kicks and spinning acrobatics. A Korean stylist took first place and I placed second.

Next, I performed a weapons kata. I placed third with a sai form that sensei Ronald Taganashi taught me. By this time I was ready for sparring. Sparring was my favorite event. My first round opponent was a six foot tall, tae kwon do stylist. He lunged towards me with a jumping round kick to the face. I side stepped his attack and countered with a flurry of rapid punches. The chief referee pulled me off of him. The judges unanimously awarded me the second point and the match. I was just starting to get warmed up. During my break between matches, I sat on the floor of the felt forum with my son Ron Jr. and Taimak.

My mentor Peter Urban taught me not to think about my opponent only what I planned to do in attacking. Fighting is taking control of the situation with explosive and creative techniques. I never really was a knock out artist. My specialty was the multiple hit system; multiple techniques delivered to several different parts of the body at the same time. Blocking and countering was the practice I learned from Bruce Lee. Rapid fire hand and leg techniques were my arsenal in sparring.

In the second round of fighting, I was matched with a real tall black brother. He was a fifth degree black belt and very skilled. Most tall men that I have fought are not used to anyone attacking them immediately with combinations. He threw a stiff reverse punch to my face. I immediately blocked and spun into a back kick to his stomach. It really knocked the wind out of him and the power of the kick knocked him out of the ring. When he came back his heart was gone. He was a beaten man mentally. My second point was a side kick to the rib cage. The chief referee raised my hand in victory. I winked at my son and bowed to the audience.

The hardest thing about tournaments is the wait between the matches. Sometimes there would be 20 or 30 fighters in the black belt division. Between matches I sat on the floor and watched the other competitors fight. It was good to see what the winners had in their arsenals. I knew that I would have to fight the winners later in the day. Sometimes you see some familiar faces but most of the time they were strangers. They all had that hungry look in their eyes. In those days my ego was so big I refused to lose. The heavyweight division was my choice of the day even though I only weighed 180 lbs. I liked fighting the big guys. All of the fighters were taller and bigger than I.

Point tournaments were fun but they were not realistic. I enjoy full contact matches like I had experienced in the orient. All the fighters wanted to beat me because I was a movie star. Most people thought I really didn't know the martial arts. They thought I was just an actor with very little martial arts skill. It seemed I always had to prove myself in life and the martial arts. Ron Jr. told me that he wanted to see more combinations in my attacks. Turn up the heat is the expression he used.

The third opponent was an old friend of mine who always wanted to compete against me. It looked as if he was going to get his wish. This fight would be different from the rest because he was a tactical fighter. He sat and watched me fight many times. He was a counter fighter like myself, and he played me like a puppet. I took the bait and attacked with a series of multiple kicking maneuvers. His counter punch hit me directly in the chest. It knocked the air out of me. I knew it was coming but didn't care. The referee awarded the first point to him He smiled at me with that overconfident smirk. The shit was on. Sometimes it is better to be scored on first to wake up the reflexes. That punch in the chest was my wakeup call. My son looked at me and shook his head. He knew the dragon was awake. Time stopped momentarily as I got my head together. U.S. Marine Corps all the way. The warrior came out full speed and with attitude.

The referee started the match again. I took a deep breath and moved in for the attack. His front kick was deflected as I punched him in the stomach and then the face. I scored on him with his favorite technique. We bowed to each other in respect. As the referee motioned the start, my opponent was moving in with a side kick to my face. The kick barely missed my face as I circled out of range. My next kick and punch combination scored on his face and stomach. The referee halted the match and declared me the winner. This being my third match, I had made it into the finals.

In the finals I had the opportunity to fight Master John Del Rio. He was a champion that easily beat his opponents with a barrage of techniques. I always wanted to fight him. As John defeated his first opponent in the finals he looked at me and pointed. He mouthed 'you are next'. The referee called me in the ring for my first final match. There is no way that I was not going to win. The match started and it looked as if my opponent was moving in slow motion. Before I knew what happened the referee was raising my arm in victory. The match was just a blur to me. Two weeks later one of my black belts gave me a copy of my fight on video. The match lasted about 30 seconds. I scored with a double punch to the face and a front kick to the stomach. It was a unanimous decision by the judges.

My next fight was for first place. In the finals you had to score three points not just two as in the eliminations. As I entered the ring, John was staring into my eyes. It was that fighter stare to break me down. He looked like he wanted to kill me. The referee looked at us and started the match. John shot in with a sidekick, crescent kick and reverse punch. I blocked and evaded his first three moves. As he closed the gap, I kicked him in the stomach with a front kick. John was holding his stomach when I kicked him in the face with a round kick. I didn't mean to hit him in the face. Hard facial contact was grounds for disqualification. After deliberation, the judges awarded me the first point of the match.

John rushed in and punched me in the face. The score was one to one. John blasted a round kick to my face. I ducked and countered with a round kick to his face. That was my second point. John was looking pissed and disappointed. I knew I couldn't give him a chance to start and attack. I had to stop him in his tracks. He was coming on like an express train, so I side stepped his kicks and countered with a side kick into his stomach. The kick catapulted him out of the ring. All four referees rushed to John's assistance. Luckily he was okay and chose to continue. Master John Del Rio is a true warrior and a real technician. Master Henry Cho presented me with the first place trophy. John gave me a hug and whispered "see you next year" in my ear. In 1989 we faced each other again with the same result. At 47 and 48 years old, I had won the All American Championship two years in a row.

Chapter31

我輩は、ロン・バン・クリフ十段

当年とって51歳

である

復活ホイス、一回戦で大会史上最年長(51歳)参加者の
ロン・バン・クリフを完全撃破!

UFC 4 at 51 years young

IN RON'S OWN WORDS

I officially retired from full contact competition in 1994 after the Ultimate Fighting Championship. The UFC was an unbelievable experience. I was 51 years of age, one month away from turning 52, when I decided to compete. I wanted to go out like a Viking with my sword in my hand. The promoters refused my first application. They said I was too old. My student Howard Niego and I went to their office with application number two. After seeing me in person they decided that I could fight in UFC IV. I started training three months before the event. My girlfriend at the time, Dorrie Ameen and her son Daoud were totally supportive of me during the training process. They made the UFC possible for me.

UFC IV is a no holds barred competition. Imagine no gloves, no weight division and no time limit. It is exciting just thinking about it. Where else could you see a boxer fight a wrestler?

My training partner, Howard Niego and I worked out together every day. The realistic fighting without gloves was mesmerizing. During my training process, black belts and wrestlers from different disciplines would come by to spar and grapple. Leon Stevenson was 270 pounds of pure muscle, standing six feet, five inches. An amazing specimen. He is fast strong and technical. At one of our sessions, Leon picked me up over his head in a suplex and dropped me on the mat. My left ankle hit the wooden frame and my ankle was broken. This happened one week before the match with Royce Gracie at UFC IV. A real bummer but I needed to fight; I was just too psyched up. After all, it was only pain. Cortisone shots and pain pills helped me make it to the octagon; the eight sided steel cage where all the action takes place.

Royce Gracie was the UFC champion three times and undefeated. Good things do come to those who have patience. When Howard, Taimak and I arrived in Tulsa, Oklahoma it was freezing. Having just come from the Cayman Islands where I was working as Chief Defensive instructor at the Royal Cayman Island Police Training Center, the brutal cold was a real shock to my body. Most of the time, I was in the hotel gym working out or promoting the event. Press conferences and interviews were held in the hotel gym.

The Pavilion Arena was sold out. The tension between the fighters was thick enough to cut with a knife. Everybody had the warrior stare. We call this the prefight psyche up. The great thing about the early UFC competitions was that you didn't know who you were fighting until the day before the event. The fight card was determined by a lottery with ping pong balls. When I picked up the ping pong ball I knew it was Royce's number. I cannot explain how happy and honored I felt. I wished for Royce and I got my wish. You know there really are miracles.

On Dec. 16, 1994 I went into my dressing room. It was utterly filthy. I laid on the floor with just a sheet between myself and the other fighters. Promoters traditionally don't have any respect for fighters. Taimak gave me a massage as I listened to Snoop Dogg, Dr. Dre and Tupac on my walkman while lying on the filthy floor.

My time had come as my crew - Howard, Taimak, Hector Santiago and Vincent Marchetti and Ira Gold hurried me to the octagon. The smoke machines were unbearable. I couldn't wait to get into the octagon. My opening round fight was with Royce Gracie. Royce is like an anaconda trying to squeeze the life out of you. Our match lasted four minutes, most of which was on the canvas. I entered the octagon first and moved to the far corner. Howard and Taimak were in my corner staring at me over the chain link fence of the octagon. Suddenly I heard the crowd start to chant, GRACIE GRACIE GRACIE. Royce and his clan were moving towards the octagon. The referee, Big John McCarthy closed the gate behind Royce. It was on!

John looked at me and said, "Are you ready!" I nodded my head. I felt like a rocket about to explode. The training had paid off, broken ankle or not. I was in the zone and facing Royce Gracie.

The lights dimmed and Big John signaled us to start. We didn't waste any time getting into action. Royce immediately moved in and threw a front kick towards my knee. I moved and side stepped the attack. As Royce reached down for my legs, I hit him with two hooks and a uppercut to the face. As he fell, the weight went down against my knee joint. My ankle collapsed and I was falling to the canvas. Right before me Royce turned into an anaconda. Wow what a rush. His punches and elbows had no effect at all. I was invincible. I felt no pain, nothing at all. I struggled in the coils of the anaconda. By the time we hit the canvas he had recovered from my combination. He felt like he weighed a thousand pounds. At one point he put his Gi top over my face to smother me. He knew all the tricks. Inch by inch he worked his way on top of me. This is called the mounted position. Royce hit me in the face and neck over a dozen times. These strikes were to distract me. His tactics and strategy worked. Eventually I turned over to evade the downward elbow strikes. At this point Royce put me in a rear naked choke. It seemed I was on the ground for an eternity. The choke was never completed because I tapped out. Better to tap out than to go to sleep. To tap out is the way an MMA fighter can avoid the inevitable. I could have resisted the choke for another minute or two but what was the point?

Royce put his fingers in my eyes to make me move my hand from the counter choke position. As long as I was holding his wrist he couldn't complete the choke. Royce was definitely in the superior position. He had leverage and technique. Luckily I pulled my other hand from under Royce to tap out. I was really pumped up. Royce is a real gentleman of quality. He is the best at what he does. Four minutes seemed like an eternity but it was all good. I did it! Big John hugged me and smiled. I bowed to Royce who then bowed to me. It was a wonderful feeling of martial arts camaraderie. Royce's father, Helio hugged me. It was a real honor for me to meet the founder of Gracie Jiujitsu. At the after fight banquet, Royce told me he couldn't believe I was 51 years old. He hoped to be in my shape when he reached my age. He was 27 and I was 51. I learned a great deal about myself from the UFC. Never quit!

When I broke my ankle I had a chance not to fight. I decided to fight anyway The Marine Corps way! Hoorah! I am eternally happy I made the right choice. Long live the Ultimate Fighting Championship. I predicted there would be a UFC 100 in 1994. Courtesy of Dana White the CEO and President of the UFC, I was at UFC 133 in Philadelphia in 2011. I will always remember the UFC as a wonderful exciting experience.

Chapter 32

Ron, Pete and our dog Rusty

IN RON'S OWN WORDS

My childhood is a blur except for the fact my mother, Doris was the best mother anyone could ever have. My brother Pete and I were inseparable as we played soldier maneuvers. He followed me every place I went. I often told my mom to tell him to leave me alone.

My mom made the best spaghetti I have ever tasted. My wife, Simina got the recipe from her. My mom would make pork chops and French fries and Pete and I would literally lick the plates.

Imagine my father was a merchant marine and almost never around. He was a decorated hero but I didn't know that side of him. I knew the hard man. During the war my father would only take ships going to the combat area, because it paid extra bonuses.

When I was a child I remember we came home from school and there on the table was a television set. It was round like a fish tank. We were the first in our neighborhood to get a television. All the neighborhood kids would come and watch TV with Pete and I. I remember seeing Elvis Presley on Ed Sullivan's show. He was an amazing performer who I mimicked. I knew and sang all of his songs. If you closed your eyes you would think he was black. Years late I met THE KING! He was being promoted by Grandmaster Ed Parker. I was there at the ceremony. The only thing I that I remember was his uniform with big collars and rhinestones in the sleeves and shoulders. He shook my hand. That was a real experience.

As a kid I would sit and read classic comic books. They were abbreviated forms of the classic tales like *A Tale of Two Cities* and *Moby Dick*. I lived in the world of comic books.

I would sit for hours drawing Disney characters like Pinocchio and Bambi. Pete would often laugh at me and make fun of me. He thought I was a silly boy. My mother Doris Williams always supported my drawing, singing and dancing. My mom believed in tough love.

When my mom was little girl, her mother died from pneumonia. Her mother's sisters took her in. She told me of the hard times. In the 1920's there was no money. She hated being poor so she did little chores and jobs to make money. There was always food but she wore only hand me downs. She would put newspaper in her shoes to fill the holes. She was very shy and innocent. Her grandfather was so strict with her.

In those days viewing of the dead took place in the living room, not a funeral parlor and this spooked my mom. She was afraid of ghosts and goblins.

Until this day she is terrified of water because her cousins used to tease and dunk her when she was a girl. She bit my uncle Freddie when he tried to dunk her at Coney Island and took a piece of meat from his shoulder. She had quite a temper. She told me many times about my cousins teasing her and pulling her hair. One day she hit one of my uncles in the head with an axe. Mom said the blood spurted out of his head. After that they didn't taunt her anymore.

I love my mother more than anything. She worked two jobs and sometimes did chores for people. Doris attended Girls' High School in Brooklyn. She met my dad, Allaire "Larry" Van Clief while she was in high school. Many times she told me that it was love at first sight. Larry was a merchant marine who was always away at sea. He was a cook and loved his job. My brother Pete and I were born premature at 7 months. My father was away at sea when we were born thinking he had nine months. Pete and I surprised everyone. My father's brother John took my mother to Unity Hospital when she was about to give birth to me. He took her into emergency and left. Uncle John was a strange one. He left without saying anything. That was the strangeness of the Van Clief's. My mom has often told me the members of the Van Clief family are the strangest people she ever saw.

I grew up in Brooklyn, New York. I have very few good memories of my dad. He was what you would call a man's man. A real tough guy who punched so hard he knocked a man out of his shoes. I couldn't believe what I saw. Doris and Larry were a real example of yin and yang, hard and soft.

Eventually after Pete and I went into the military she left him. When Dad died of a drug overdose she was not living with him. My Aunt Sarah and Aunt Edy called my mom at her job and asked her to stop by after she came from work. My mom went to Herkeimer Street where Aunt Sarah lived. Aunt Sarah asked her to sit down. She sensed something was wrong. When they told her she thought I am finally free. She went to the city morgue to identify his body the next day.

In all those years I never ever remember my father telling me that he loved me. I tell Kai I love him every day as I did his brother Ron Jr. I didn't want to be like that. In all my years I have always loved kids. When I was a teenager, I taught dances such as the Twist and the Monkey to all the neighborhood kids.

When Pete and I were living at 2155 Dean Street in Brooklyn our bikes were taken by two boys who lived in our same building. We lived on the second floor and they lived on the ground floor. I remember their mother's name was Ethel. She kicked and banged our apartment door and was screaming very loud. Pete and I were hiding behind our mother. When my mother opened the door she pushed my mother in the face. Her mistake. My mom reached back and picked up a baseball bat and hit her in the head. The blood poured from the woman's head. Later that day my father went down to their apartment and banged on the door to talk with the man of the house. He threatened that man's life. The man opened the door and slid our bikes out. Those were some of my memories of growing up in Brooklyn with my mother.

I could never tell her anything that happened to me in the military. I was ashamed and guilty for some of the things I was ordered to do. Even now, to this day I will never forgive myself. How can I? They say you never get cured from post traumatic stress disorder, you just learn how to cope with it. Coping skills are the key to my survival. When I came home from Vietnam my mind was lost. Many years have passed since then and those memories have never left me. They will never leave me.

Chapter 33

My parents - Allaire and Doris Van Clief

IN RON'S OWN WORDS

My mother Doris told me in 2011 that she had never met anyone that had been married as many times as me. I said "Mom I believe in love and am a total romantic." Why would someone get married six times if they didn't believe in true love? Richard Pryor and I often joked about the advantages and disadvantages of multiple marriages.

My first wife, Rene Gaines was a beautiful African American airline stewardess and Chinese goju black belt. My mind was much too damaged to be a good husband. Unfaithful and self centered were my major problems. I lived only for the martial arts. At that time I didn't know how much damage was incurred in the military experience.

My second wife, Milagros Tirado was a Puerto Rican and the mother of my first son Ron Jr. aka Shihan. I really couldn't relate to anything but the martial arts and was consumed by it. I trained 6 a.m. to 10 p.m. at the dojo every day. She left me when Ron Jr. was three and I became a single parent. One of the most liberating and learning experiences of my life was becoming a single parent.

My third wife, Laura Rappa was an Italian-American trapeze artist and circus performer. She was fascinating and one of the most physically fit women I have ever met. Laura and I worked on her trapeze act together. I trained as a catcher not a flyer. She was a tyrant and trained daily. We travelled the globe with circus companies. When I fell and injured my neck and shoulder, my career as a flyer was over. Our marriage was broken by her family's racist attitudes. Laura was pregnant and was beaten up by one of her family members. She told me she lost the baby. This totally destroyed our relationship.

My fourth wife, Kim Hardiman was a Chinese American kung fu artist, art teacher and dancer. We broke up in the Cayman Islands about a year after our marriage. I stayed in the Cayman Islands training the police department.

My fifth wife was Tamara Sienicka, a Polish American and a very special lady. Tamara had been a ballet dancer in her youth and a naturalist. Health food and clean living was her mantra. She was a wonderful woman although tough as nails. Tamara and my mother were good friends. Tamara died of a brain tumor in 2005.

My sixth wife Simina Prohor, a Romanian, is a super athlete, basketball player, coach and mother of my son, Kai. Simina made me realize that love was still alive in me. Before Simina I was dead inside for decades; just going through the motions not feeling, just being. She is a special woman with a heart of gold. She is from the same tough breed as my mother. They don't make women like them anymore.

Finally let me say that love is real. We all need love to survive. There is nothing better than the love of your family and friends. Without love we are dead. I was dead for decades until I found Simina. Thank you sweetheart for helping me to realize that I could still feel love. People say I am crazy marrying six times. I am not and never will be afraid of failure. Don't you think I deserve to be happy and married? I love being a father and husband. I will believe in love and marriage until the day I die. I would get married 100 times to find the right woman. There is nothing more wonderful than the love of a man, a woman and a child. It is love that keeps us alive like the blood in our veins and the air in our lungs. So you see I really am a total romantic. I wouldn't want to have it any other way. Love is forever!

Chapter 34

RONALD VAN CLIEF
2155 Dean Street Brooklyn
N. Y. J.H.S. 178.
The face that sunk a thousand
ships.

Ron's High School Yearbook Photo

IN RON'S OWN WORDS

Boys' High School was the best school in Brooklyn. They had the best football, basketball, swimming and gymnastics teams in the nation. I attended Boys' High because it was not a co-ed school. I wanted only to train and get stronger for my tour in the United States Marine Corps. I didn't want any distractions. I was very shy around girls.

I was a member of the Boys' High School Leader Corps. The Leader Corps was an elite group of gymnastics experts. Like yesterday, I remember Mr. Heft giving me my red and black school colored tee shirt. I was so very proud. We were the best that Boy's High had to offer. My specialties were the horizontal bar, parallel bars, rings and floor routines.

One day I was practicing my giant swing in the gym. As I revolved around the bar, my grip loosened and I was thrown about 20 feet in the air. I fell on my back on the basketball court floor, 15 feet away from the bar. When I became conscious my cousin Kirk was standing above me laughing From that day forward I always used chalk on my hands before I got on to any apparatus.

My gym teachers, William Heft and Phil Cox, really supported and assisted me in becoming a physical fitness addict. I will always remember them with respect and admiration. Years later Mr. Heft became the manager of the world famous Madison Square Garden. Mr. Cox became the principal of the 'The High' decades later. Actually Boys' High became Boys and Girls High School and moved to Fulton Street in Brooklyn. My days at the High will always be some of the fondest memories of my life. To this day I can remember some of the words to the school song.

The legendary professional basketball star Connie Hawkins was one of my schoolmates. One time Connie was talking to Vaughn Harper (who later became a famous national radio celebrity on WBLS) and I tied Connie's shoe laces together. Connie started to walk away and he tripped and fell like a big redwood tree. All my classmates were hysterical. Connie wanted to really kick my ass but I was too fast for him. A few days later I saw Connie in the gym. He had his sneakers hanging around his neck by the laces. When he saw me I bolted. He threw his sneakers at me and they wrapped around my legs. It was like a gaucho throwing his bolos at an ostrich. I fell down on my face. When I looked up, Connie was standing over me laughing his ass off. I started to laugh at myself. Connie and Vaughn were celebrities at the High. I knew they would become famous someday because they were so extraordinary.

Lou Wilson, member of the rock and roll group Mandrill, was one of my classmates at the High. We are the boys of BHS you've heard so much about. The people stop and stare at us whenever we go out. We're noticed for the clever things we do. Those were some of the most wonderful days of my life growing up in Brooklyn.

I lived at 2155 Dean Street, at the corner of Saratoga avenue, next door to JHS 178. In 2007, I went to see my old dwelling. It has become a drug rehab and residential treatment center. High School 178 was still next door almost exactly as I remembered it.

In my early teenage years I would go up on the roof and sing the Drifters classic 'Up On The Roof' which was my favorite song. This song gave me hope to someday find true love. In life all we have is memories - good and bad ones. I now know how to create those good memories. I have learned many things about this existence we call life. Survival is the strongest component of the human DNA. I am no longer the 18 year old virgin who loved nothing better than to sit and draw cartoons and read Shakespeare.

My United States Marine Corps experience changed my entire life, never to be the same again. The innocent young boy died one night in 1963. I am a different person today. We can only try to become better in living life. I really sat back and watched my life pass. A people watcher. Now I am an active participant in living the life I want. Every day is a challenge. Challenge yourself to do something that takes you out of your comfort zone. It is liberating. Be the best you can be for yourself so that you can be of benefit to others.

My mentor, Dr. Peter G. Urban said to me thousands of times 'ZEN is Zeal Energy and Nowness'. I think he meant Z is for zeal the mental pshychophysical drive engaged for maximum human potential. Energy is the mind, spirit and body result. When you relax and feel your energy force and can control it, that is the true benefit of martial arts experience. Nowness is the perspective of living in the right now. Today is Now! Don't Quit!

Chapter 35

The Black Dragon - Victory Comics 2012

IN RON'S OWN WORDS

Growing up in Brooklyn, every neighborhood had their bullies. Pecos was the neighborhood bully who stood 6' 6" tall at about 260 pounds. He lived across the street from me. Pecos terrorized all the kids. He was always beating somebody up. This day I guess it was my day for the beating. As soon as he saw me, the chase began. I ran down into the basement of the building that I lived in. He was right behind me. I climbed down under the coal chute and out the back door into the backyard. Pecos was right behind me cursing and reaching. I jumped onto a chain link fence and climbed over. He was fat and couldn't follow me. I laughed and taunted him. Pecos disappeared through a hole in the fence and there he was between me and the high school behind me. I cut and ran behind me not knowing it was a dead-end. Behind me were the brick walls of JHS 178. Over top of an entrance door was my escape hatch. It was two parallel walls that faced each other so that I could climb up the 25 foot wall to safety. Like Spiderman I used the force and strength of my arms and legs to scale the wall. Pecos was standing below me with that angry face shaking his fist. I disappeared like a ninja. Actually I did the same scaling stunt on the other side of the wall to get down. I escaped across the roof of the lunch room. The next day I saw Pecos and he winked at me and smiled.

After my cousin Kirk threatened his life, Pecos and I became friends until his death in 2003. Pecos, rest in peace. Pecos was an army veteran who served in Vietnam as an airman. From the 1970's to 2003 he spent his time in a wheel chair and on crutches living in a basement boiler room apartment. In 2003, I called him and was told he had died of a massive heart attack. He really was a nice guy who loved his gin and juice. Over the years I would visit him, sit back and smoke a joint and reminisce. Pecos was like the mayor of Brooklyn. Everybody knew him as Crazy Pecos. I knew him as my friend.

Chapter 36

Boys High School - Brooklyn, New York

IN RON'S OWN WORDS

The Blue Jackets were a paramilitary organization with an army/marine philosophy that trained teenagers in life classes. Camping and military games were very common. I was 12 years old when I met Commander Vaughn who took an immediate interest in me. He was an ex-marine drill instructor who served and was decorated in Korea. He taught me the manual of arms, the gold standard of boot camp weapons presentation. It looked like it was being done by a robot. Each movement was precise and strong. Commander Vaughn knew I was preparing to go to boot camp and he was going to get me ready.

War games were my favorite. Like John Wayne I was always the hero. When we used the pugilsticks I became a different person. I wanted to destroy my enemy. As a pre-teenager I was being taught to be a professional soldier/killer. Commander Vaughn was a crack shot and qualified as an expert marksman by the United States Marine Corps.

Kirk and I joined together but he quit early in the program. I was in heaven. Marching, saluting and drills. The bean bag fights and chalk bag training was honing my skills with the knife, bayonet and rifle. I particularly liked the pugilsticks, it was the only place I felt in control of the opponent. Because of my gymnastics and martial arts background I was molded into a professional fighting machine.

Overnight hikes and camping with sleeping bags was a great break from the tenement life that I knew. Survival training was right up my alley. I was born for it! I credit the Blue Jackets and Commander Vaughn in particular for molding me at an early age in the art of war. For getting me ready, so I thought, for Marine Corps Boot Camp. I was wrong. Nothing in the world could have prepared me for Parris Island. Thank you Commander wherever you are. I believe everyone should have some military training as a foundation for life.

Chapter 37

Ron at UFC on December 16, 1994 in Tulsa, Oklahoma

I remembered that I'd made a promise to somebody, somewhere, at some time but I couldn't remember who, nor if I really ever made one to begin with. Paranoia flew up in a cloudy gust of perspiration slapping me so hard in the face settling me down again to ride on the back of the Black Dragon. And he never did it for anybody else but himself. His father was a monster and we are all monsters. You can't do anything for a monster but lock him up or put him down and the two of them never made their peace. And there was never peace again; the smell of an old dirt road, the wind in the parking lot, street lamps and headlights, the news and the history, racism and slavery – all words with the letters of the alphabet. They are all forward in their contempt for each other debating over whose first second and third; which one of them will be the body. There're favorites, but most of them are pawns to takes point for the king.

When did he ever listen? The whole point of being king is to escape the chitter chatter. He needs time to think and build the kingdom. But the burden of the emperor is that he must look after his people, for their hardships soon become his misfortunes and civilizations are toppled because of a few words that got left out. Was the fight for you or for somebody else? Could they see where this was going?

A teardrop of rain split the gorge of drought. Somewhere in the universe, time stood still as a universe inside it suddenly appeared. War trained men this way; to deal with the mental turbine of extraterrestrial interference. The two universes collide and the byproduct became the year 2010; a space oddity. Everything that had been seen or could be imagined showed up clear in the diamond sphere. Life was a movie flashing before your eyes; pretty pictures of heaven for you to pick and glue together. The trick was keeping it all together. Man cannot shelter himself with newspaper. Those words are black and the blood runs quick in the rain. Better to move to the mountains and build yourself a cabin. Burn those words to heat your kindling.

I needed solitude. I needed to be alone so that I could retake myself and fuck the world all night long with a case of 50 Euro notes. Life was all about its ups and downs. Ron showed me the gun he put in his mouth. I asked him to leave the room. I didn't need to look inside his eyes for this. The steel was cold beneath my grip. I took the pistol firmly like I always do and popped the canister. There was one round inside the chamber; forty years later.

The room around me changed. The walls were painted yellow. There was a thin cotton blanket on the bed in the corner, a bookshelf and a table.

'So this is how I get my thrill?' I thought.

I spun the canister around the chamber, cocked the hammer and swallowed. The site on the end of the barrel cut the roof of my mouth. My tongue licked up against the gun-oily steel. I had to think real hard to stop and couldn't find a reason. The trigger pulled a click, then a knock at the door and Ron came in the room.

"Yeah. I know. So just write this book mother fucker," Ron called out on the telephone. I hadn't seen him in half a year. He was calling between Stress Inoculation Training and PTSD Therapy with the Doctors at the VA hospital in New Jersey. I don't know what the hell he was doing back there. When I left, he lost it. We pulled out everything from his mind in a matter of weeks and then I left. There was no closure on anything, just like he said and he'd gone off the deep end again into a great depression.

"It's too much brother. I have to share a room with a guy who can't sleep without the lights on. These guys are screaming in their sleep. I haven't slept in three weeks. They got me in here so sedated, talking to the shrinks trying to deal with all of this."

Was it my taste of freedom? I felt like I missed so much before. Even though my body started breaking there was never too much pain I could not endure. The bullet hit me strong. The flirtation with death brought about the strangest bedfellows. Day turned into night and ten years turned into a day. I'd long since forgotten about the Black Dragon and here he was again, broken again like the past I'd heard about. My beard was to my chest and flies buzzed around my mat of natty locks. The rags on me had once been the finest white linen. I'd had them tailored in Portugal. I met a fine older lady there who asked me about her pearls. I told her they were worth nothing. She should give them to me as a favor I did insist on helping them to the trash.

Two months later I was eating some kind of meat in a brown sauce on a side street somewhere in Thailand. I smuggled 200k into the country and left it with a friend of mine whose father traded jade. I gave him specific instructions to make a weekly payment of two thousand dollars to the opium den I'd checked into. I wanted to taste my last meal before the endless orgy. It could have been dog I was chewing on. It all tasted like chicken.

I woke up several months later on the side of the road in the same clothes you find me in now. So let me ask you while you're curious. What is the hypotenuse of an isosceles triangle?

"Hey boss, can you spare me a dollar?"

I was slapped so hard in the back of the head. The Dragon snapped me with his tail while I was dreaming. He woke me and we flew again into a different morning.

"Do you hear me Sparky? They've got me locked up in the VA Hospital with all these nut jobs and I'm trying to keep from killing everybody. I've had three tranquilizers today and all I can see is sitting in that fucking helicopter mowing people down. You gotta help me, brother.

"The WOMA has honored me with a doctorate degree in self defense and philosophy. I don't want any awards or degrees. They don't have any meaning to me."

He didn't sound right. I wanted to believe him, but where was he? He was in a mental hospital? "So how are you feeling?" I asked.

"Fucked up, man. I can't find me chick anywhere. She was waiting for me to get off work. I was cleaning my M-16 machine gun and put it back in my locker, then went out and to get some booty. Right? Three dollars a hit, man. How can you lose on that?"

"That's great."

"I have a pussy bill going in town."

"In New York?" I asked. I was confused. "Even if they were five dollars, you still can't beat that," I said.

"They give me more than five dollars worth. I feel like I paid a thousand dollars. I've already caught the clap three times."

"Are you out of your mind?"

"Of course...it's just the clap," he said. "I had the clap once, twice, maybe three times. I had syphilis once. What do you expect? These chicks are fucking a hundred guys a week. You do the math. I'm at Suckahachi Alley. You just put your dick through the screen and they'll work it for you; one dollar."

"What are you talking about...Vietnam? I thought you said you were in New York? Do they even still have Suckahachi Alley?"

"Of course. Man, these drugs are wild. They got me on more pills in this place than a pharmacy, man. We're doing some major therapy."

I lit a spliff. I rolled it with a little opium that I got from a next door neighbor. As I was speaking I was going comatose. Smoking opium is like smoking a thousand joints and topping it off with some acid. That's what it is. You can't move. After a few pokes you're there. It makes the difference between trying to write a song as a beginning musician and the Grateful Dead. The Grateful Dead wrote about things they knew rather than what they tried to know.

Just because we were put under the restraints, we had an idea and we went with it. Most people just talk about the push. Anyone can collaborate and then it doesn't work. Maybe I shouldn't have asked so many questions, but if he would have put the gun in his mouth and finally pulled the trigger, the book would be a best seller. I didn't wish that upon anybody and I didn't care about fame like that. I wanted my friend. We were caught in a parallel universe with nowhere to go. My mind was shot from the opium spliff. I just sat back and wrote.

I could see Ron smiling. He would say, 'Send it in to the Writer's Guild. I'll make sure the money is right. You'll have to trust me on this'. I trusted him completely. We were going to make enough money that neither one of us would ever have to worry about money for at least a while. 'Go to L.A. take some screenwriting courses 'You'll stay out there and write for one of those companies. Get your foot in deep. Take your shovel out and dig that motherfucking trench and that's it. That's where I want to leave you' he said. I didn't know if that was where I wanted to be left, but I trusted him. The book was just another vehicle. We would go for film rights, video games, action figures, lunch boxes; all of it.

Chapter 38

Department of Veteran Affairs
Diploma; March 25, 2011

I could see Ron in his music therapy classes in the hospital. His mind was broken. The doctors at the Veteran's hospital kept him going from 7:30 in the morning until 5:00 every night. I managed to get a hold of him between his 'Feelings Group' and the 'Seeking Safety Group Therapy'.

I had a fight in Russia. A bare knuckle match. Somebody had paid me enough money and a plane ticket to fly my ass over to St. Petersburg and go into the cage with some Ukrainian war criminal.

"Don't do it," he said. "You could get killed. They don't have cage fights yet."

"The referee will break it up before any damage is done and there's too much blood."

"The referees don't give a fuck in Russia," he told me. "I saw a guy stomped in the neck and killed in Russia at a show and the prize money wasn't shit. It was like thirty grand in an eight man absolute tournament. I don't know how many millions of rubles that is. A guy got killed for that. There are three million people living in the subways in St. Petersburg. Russian winters are not like New York or Montana. They're harsh, very harsh. It's one of the few places in the world I travelled a lot and never really liked. The quality of life for regular people is appalling."

"I need the money."

"You don't need the money and you'll get killed anyway."

It was true. They were still developing a UFC kind of organization in Eastern Europe. Ron had already travelled to Yugoslavia, Poland, Ukraine and Russia. The people were not living well. They didn't have quality of life. There is rich and there is poor. There is no middle class. Just like the United States is today. Everybody looked like they were from Transylvania. Their skin was pale; their teeth malnourished. I met some amazing athletes coming out of Romania. Ron's wife, Simina was one of those gifted multi sport players. In those days Romania ruled Olympic gymnastics competition.

Every place you go people are smoking cigarettes, pipes and cigars. Eastern Europe takes you back in time like a time shuttle. The buildings and streets so dark green and grey reminds me of the wars fought. They have so many military museums and concentration camp sites it is a little overbearing.

"Just finish the book."

I'd forgotten about the book completely. I'd been stoned for several months now. I'd forgotten to take a shower and my beard went long. I only trained to fight. That was all I could wrap my head around. I listened to what Ron was saying. He was fighting his own demons. I don't know if they were his or if they were mine and we were both living the same mind. I heard one of us say, "Besides, the food is too salty and every place you go, mother fuckers are smoking cigarettes. Everybody is smoking all the time and drinking gin, scotch, rum or whatever they're drinking. They're always smoking and drinking. That's too much for me. I can't take it anymore."

The hospital was really getting to him. He started to cry into the phone. "One of the marines overdosed on heroin and went into a coma. He died shortly after that. His belly was so big they had to build an extra section on the coffin to go around his belly. Have you ever seen that before? I'd never seen it either. The coffin is the regular rectangle with an extra box around the belly part. His belly was like it didn't belong to him. The booze got to him and all the shit they make you confront. They put us right back in the middle of that fucking LZ."

Very few people have the chance in their martial arts training to study with five or ten Grand Masters. You can't even dream that. I couldn't dream about it now. I was too stoned. I wanted to be a Kung Fu master like the Black Dragon. What the fuck did I know about anything? I took a lot of LSD after I met Ron so I could relate to the world he spoke of. I don't remember how many trips I took, but it was more than I could count. I must have talked to Johnny Depp at least five times in the mirror.

"You had to go through the hell first. I realize that. I see a lot of that in Johnny Depp. He's such a diverse character."

"You got to get yourself together," a voice echoed inside my head. I felt like I was in the loony bin.

"He's one of the most brilliant actors out there," Ron offered. "I met him in Paris one time. What a beautiful person; no ego. He's just a down brother, really nice. I told you when I first met Sam he said, 'I know who you are'. 'Really?' I asked. 'You're the Black Dragon'. Damn, you know? I used to go to Forty Deuce and see movies and run into guys like Richard

Pryor. When they tell you something like that it's hard to comprehend. You've got what it takes. Don't let it go and don't let the drugs get you into a place you can't get out of. I'm telling you honest. When a person like Richard Pryor walks up to you in real life it makes the world that much smaller, or bigger I guess. That's what makes it scary. It doesn't really scare me. It just is what it is. Listen to me. We are going to make this happen. We are going to make this movie happen. We are going to make this book happen. We are going to make this happen and as soon as I get out of this place we'll be sitting on the beach in Hawaii. You'll be Armani down to the toe and I'll be Gucci'd down and what not. We're going to do it. And it's not going to be just one of these things. I'm telling you now. This is my warning to you. We're going to do a lot of them."

"Right on, Man. I wish you could hit this shit."

"Get yourself together, because it's going to happen. It's the ride. It's the adventure. I've come to a place on my own after setting out on the adventure. I set out on the adventure and during it I found where I should go back to make my roots again, to carry on again and run with it. Then I get to this place. What lies ahead is the next part of the journey. Had I not gone on the adventure in the first place, I wouldn't be able to go further with you. That's just life. I wish there was a choice but there isn't. I got you on this road and now I'm on this road too. I've got to go back to Hollywood; suits and ties, radio shows, television talk shows and light up all those shadows. I'm telling you where we're going to be. When it's time to rock and roll, I'm going to call you up and let you know your ticket is waiting at the check in counter at the airport. That's all. Believe me. I won't make any deal unless I run it past you first regarding our book. I think you should have the option to tell me what you think. Stop smoking that shit and get me some pages I can work with. The people from California emailed me today. They're going to let me know when they're ready to start filming the next segment for the Black Kung Fu Experience. I told you I did some episodes for the Black Kung Fu Show? They sold it to the PBS channel and I'm going to be the host. I'm going to be doing a lot of that, at least 24 shows. We'll film in Hollywood, Chicago, Japan, China, and the Philippines. It's going to be everywhere. They're going to highlight black kung fu artists all over the world. It's going to be huge."

Too bad though, because of economics the series became one film to be seen on PBS...I guess something is better than nothing. It was a very interesting project that Ron was honored to participate in.

Chapter 39

Ron, Simina and Kai Van Clief

I could really go for a Band-Aid. Where do we go from here? That was the question I was faced with. My body was numb and I couldn't sleep. I was fighting in a war where I couldn't see the enemy coming. He was scattered in snippets across the world spoken about at tables and street corners. To be thought of so, was the disturbing distraction playing on people's minds. I could feel it in my chest. The 'it' clawed its way into my heart...forgive me. In my sane mind I left the eye becoming this man so typical of how men should be.

I learned to live again in the mind of another. I fought because I was a fighter. Not even the drink inspired me, thirsty from the first wake in the morning for the challenging opposition. After that, I proceeded upon moral inebriation twixt the vice and the turnkey. There were miles to go and I couldn't; trapped inside by the lie in my own mind with the belief I created that I might escape from the common life and be free to look around the heavens. For the religious, anecdotal proclaims and afterlife of such illustrious proclivities. Perhaps redundant and then I saw that it was all that way; luxurious grand. Man in his primal dominion sought for nothing less than what he knew to be true, never tell.

"Show me your baby bird," I told a girl as she walked by, "for I haven't got the time to be wasted on thoughts of what I'd like to do. I'll put you crackers in a box and save you for later when I'm putting the dog to bed. Cursed all of you bloody wankers. I don't have time for ye."

My heart almost exploded and I couldn't see my finger when I tried to touch it, it wasn't where. I was alone again. The opium was wearing off and shook me from my body and my legs wouldn't work. I had gone into the infinite reality. How could I ever look back? I was short of breath.

Ron's spoken word was less than…well anything you can imagine. He could say anything if he was put on the spot.

Page after page after page until my mind bled; running the pages dry. I couldn't go on forever. I'd have to know that I was not. Was it a dream or a nightmare? I could not see the sun anymore. It was a gamble I made with society because they'd forgotten to hold on. People didn't feel it anymore. They couldn't taste the air they breathed, sometimes left speechless imagining the things that are possible and every man is an island floating in a sea of toxicity. It comes from the very bottom of the heart with the deepest sincerity and love for all of existence that we do speak at all.

To call it what it is shows the blasphemy of our ignorance. We are all not in one box. We are all in boxes; a world of Legos. He was a black man now travelling around the world on a five film deal. Back to Ghana where he once laid his hat and started over with the boy. Ghana was a long time ago. Waikiki sounded much nicer. He had a smile on his face. What a magnificent kingdom sprawled before us. What a magnificent will he passed on to us with persuasion and surrender. Search for the tenderness that one has so abandoned.

Romance was in a pinky hold tapping out to the pornography of an overwhelming seductress. None of it made sense. Could the editors put together the imagination of one man's mind, turning it into the creation of everything? You on the other side who listens across the ocean; who breathes hiding behind your walls; who suggests of knowing anything about something; how could you with a lost voice that's been silenced tell me that things would work out?

Did we speak those which were the best words or did we put together a diatribe to use against the rest of the world running on words; the mind of Ron van Clief. Is that what you wanted; the life story of him living in torment and suffering; looking over his shoulder every day of his life not knowing what's coming after him. He does not enjoy the chance of reveling in the music of the Beatles perhaps; so that the rest of us could listen to Sergeant Pepper's Lonely Hearts Club Band. He's got Staff Sergeant Smokey Stover yelling in his brain as he takes his medicine every day at the VA Hospital. He walks. He doesn't drive, always wearing shorts and a backpack over his shoulders ready to take on this world as he's always done better than the rest of us. He was truly a superhero walking among us and we didn't even see him. But he is there. We are here to do what we must do. To see what we must see beyond our imagination…life in the third world in the manifestations of our own creation…talking about it over and over until we confuse ourselves with it and it's confusing.

With the bubble around me, I shield myself with the graces of my mind so that we can all follow the trail of the Black Dragon. The world does not surprise me but so many die for a cause other than the one that is to be lived today. It was all a conspiracy in the first place. When was it ever real? He was searching for the paper to write it all down on. He couldn't search forever.

There just wasn't the time and even if he had the time he wouldn't.

All I need is paper…one hundred sheets did not inspire him. The junior legal pad; what, were they messing with him? One day left and then off to the races…off to the hands of the critics who would dictate his future holding his mind in whatever grips or lock they could capture; squeezing him, bonding him with the glue that held his brain together.

Pay me more. Pay me more. It wasn't even about the money because he could never make as much money as he wanted to tossing rocks for somebody else. Just give me some Goddamn paper. He saw it; the sketchbook on the bottom third shelf. Paper mate 1.0 mm. What did that mean; that is was fatter than a crayon? This was not a children's story…point o'seven, the pilot. That was a good back up. What was wrong with this store? They'd stopped buying products from Asia. It was only made in America. The Velocity Gel 0.7 and it was even less than the Pilot. He couldn't go wrong with a Bic. Without even skipping a beat he walked to the cash register passed the stock boy with the shopping cart taking out boxes to the trash in the alley.

"Hi, how are you?"

The cashier didn't utter a word. She scanned the pen and the sketchpad through the synthetic sapphire laser beeping several times as I gave her a 20 and she punched in the numbers to give me my change. Thirteen forty two.

"Thank you."

"Good night."

That was it. No, how are your folks? How's the family? The parking lot was empty. There was more space than he could run in a day in front of him. He couldn't see the ocean. That was for damn sure. He couldn't find the keys to a car that would run. He shouldn't be driving. They were in his pocket. It was a story. Somebody opened up their mouth one day and words were written down as they were heard. Could he only ever be there on it? Were any of them not? The Mescaline worked inside of him. Where did he get that?

The year was 1973 again; Hong Kong. His mind was cooking. He put it in reverse. Where was he going? Something terrible had happened. He saw through his hand to the steering wheel and again he was driving. The ring of eternal life had escaped his finger. He gave it up for he knew she was his lover and there could never be another for this was the way of superheroes. This was the decision; the split; the now or never; the make or break.

If it doesn't happen she's leaving you. If you don't publish, she's gone. So, do what you will people who put their heads together. Tell us what to think. Tell us what to do. He'd gotten so far off track perhaps he was never coming back. Where was the Black Dragon now? Where was his hero when he needed him? Where were his hopes and dreams that were speaking to him? Where was he? He was in space talking to himself; where nobody would listen. How could they? It was all rambling. Everything! How could they make me a hero? I just wanted to ride on the back of the Dragon. He'd beaten them. They'd beaten him and he was not afraid anymore. They were the cowards and the weak and he loved them because they were him.

He let them get to his head and when he'd had enough of them they were gone again. There was so much peace he wanted to show. You know that's all he wants. To raise his son in a world without problems which he knows is impossible to shield any kind of the truth. At 9:51 on May 10, 2010, a light in the darkness turned on. A glimpse of hope once again broke free. A rectangle showed in the black abyss, miles in front of his giant retinas. If it were only miles, he imagined, by the time I get there I'd see the sun again. The day is now upon us when we can be free. A pitcher of water and a loaf of bread in wax paper came through the light.

"I don't want it," he screamed breaking off into whisper. "But thank you all the same." When he spoke the words there was a cactus in the desert mirage of the tiny rectangle and he took it and he shrunk himself to the size of humility starting to walk towards the light saying, "thank you for all you've done for me."

Even the pen came with a plastic tip. He took a fresh sheet of paper and started writing. There were only hours left on the deadline. He was going up against 100,000 of them at once; a reasonable number as there was no need to exaggerate.

On the mountain above the clouds the air was thinner and euphoria overwhelmed the senses of our imagination. The Black Dragon flew around the sky with a calm smile and kind eyes, for a man will understand humility if he lives long enough having carried his weight in this world.

It was down to the raw; the nitty gritty. He finally had time for it, but there was little time left. The Mescaline turned the dragon's layer into the hills of another world where grandchildren and loved ones exist; a sense of time in the confusion of worth and value.

Ron's mind was never still. There were a million places to be and more to do and we all could do all of it if we stopped telling ourselves why we couldn't. The truth was he was by himself. He'd tried to start over not knowing there are no do-overs. The women from the forest offered him a strawberry and he could not refuse the fresh fruit.

"Thank you," he said delighted. "And would you mind telling me, which way to Everland."

"Sorry Chap. We haven't heard that one before. Could you help us out with it?"

"Come, I'll help you. I think it's this way."

He took them from paradise to something real because he wasn't meant for anything else. He could write a scene. He could write a play. He would write his own legacy one day. It was non-fiction and it was the essence of what the Black Dragon combats every day of his life; towering down from the sky to never do their dirty work again.

I've seen him when we really got down to the cruel nature of human beings. He always laughed whenever Kai was around. If you ever wanted to quit, then you could save yourself the good-bye, because the Black Dragon would be gone faster than a little boy could imagine growing up. Don't say you don't believe in Black Dragons for they do exist.

Kai was a mighty warrior from a far off land and he came to claim his throne, seeing that it had always been his, the dragon. His dragon. The young prince patted his dragon on the back and they were off among the clouds far above the land called limitation.

"You can never chain me." He smiled. "You can never kill me." The young prince screamed brandishing his sword.

The Black Dragon screeched a shrilling horror across the lands down below. Go on forever Black Dragon. We will slay them in the fields below and they swooped down low on Sunset Blvd. where the Black Dragon smashed down on top of a limousine escorting somebody to the red carpet premier of the movie. We smiled and laughed and went inside.

Never quit! No matter what happens. Never quit on yourself! Take a deep breath and slowly let it out…Keep going!

My Life in Images

Ron fights at 51 years old in UFC IV

Pain and Pride

241

Ron fighting Joe Richardson with Chaka Zulu in chair on the right

My life in images

Ron with Richard Pryor

RON VAN CLIEF
Headshot 1985

Pete Van Clief

Ron and his son Kai on Sapphire Beach

Ron with good friend Gregory Hines

Ron and cousin Kirk Wood

Parris Island February, 1961

Ron with Dean Brockway in 1981

Ron and Simina at Ross Kaye's wedding

**Ron Jr aka Shihan the poet at 6 years old
doing aikijitsu 1981**

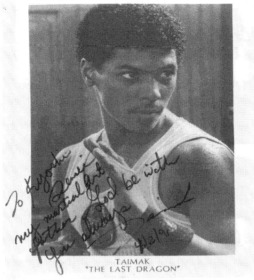

TAIMAK
"THE LAST DRAGON"

My martial arts son, Taimak Guariello 1981-2002 The journey from student to master Chinese Goju Forever

Still from the movie *The Death of Bruce Lee* starring Ron Van Clief

The Manual of Martial Arts, written by
Ron Van Clief became a New York
Times Best Seller in the 1980s

Official RON VAN CLIEF poster

*There are things called Dragons
That ride the clouds and walk the winds.
And Ron...
You are the closest thing
to a mutha-fuckin' Dragon
alive ever seen —*

Louis Venosta

Louis Venosta wrote cult classic *The Last Dragon*

Wing Tsun hqtrs Koowloon Hong Kong GM Leung Ting School 1973

Feeling the glow 1974

**Lance Corporal Ron Van Clief USMC
3rd Marine Division**

The Black Dragon movie poster

Ron with Berry Gordy on the set of *The Last Dragon* 1984

Ron at 65 years young

**Ronnie and Cousin June sitting on the steps of JHS178
Rusty was my dog**

The cover of *BLACK HEROES OF THE MARTIAL ARTS*
with Taimak Guariello *The Last Dragon* 1996

Ron and Mr. George Benson

Brooklyn brothers Iron Mike Tyson and Ron in Las Vegas

Young Dragon and The Last Dragon

Ron the Commissioner of the Ultimate Fighting Championship at work - UFC 5

Ron and David Hasselhoff at UFC 6   David told me I had balls of steel to fight in UFC 4. David was an early UFC fan who believed in the sport. He is a superstar of stage, screen and television

Absolute Unconditional Love: Ron and Kai day 1

Dr. Maya Angelou and Ron Van Clief

Ron and Michael Jai White

Ron and Ron Jr., Shihan on homestead rooftop in lower Manhattan's east village homestead

Ron, Karriem Abdallah, Wesley Snipes and Ronald Duncan

The Chinese Goju Virtues

CHINESE GOJU is my secret, I bear no arms. May God help me if I ever have to use my Art.

1. Love is our Law.
2. Truth is our Worship.
3. Form is our Manifestation.
4. Conscience is our Guide.
5. Peace is our Shelter.
6. Nature is our Companion.
7. Order is our Attitude.
8. Beauty and Perfection is our Life.

My Virtues

The Hanged Man

The Monkey climbs

Ron at 69 years young. Martial fitness is my life.

Mike Carro assists Ron with self defense 2011

Harnessing the chi power in kata performance

We all share the same pain. The brothers of Lyons VA Hospital combat PTSD veterans preparing for the trip to the wall in Washington, DC. I was having panic attacks and severe anger management issues...On the bus ride stops, I would do kata in the parking lot with the vets who were training with me. John Holcolme, Mike Carro, Ron Brooks, Tom, Rasool, Fitz - you guys helped me so much and to Sonny Sabine a stand up guy, thank you.

261

Simina Van Clief my wife, my love and
Kai's mother.

Ron Van Clief Japan Exposition World Karate Championship
1st place heavyweight black belt and Grand Champion 1969

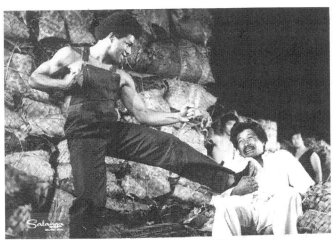

The Black Dragon in the Philippines

BLACK DRAGON THE LEGEND OF RON VAN CLIEF

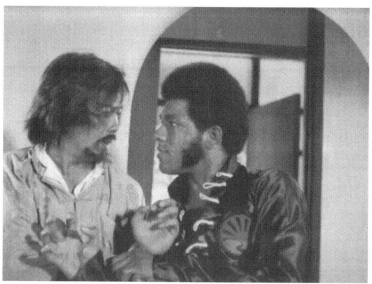

The Death of Bruce Lee aka *The Black Dragon's Revenge* starring Ron Van Clief

New Martial Arts Magazine 1974. Ron Van Clief and Charles Bonet

Regis and Ron

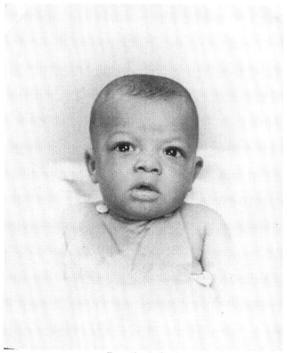

Ron the infant

Ron Van Clief, Dr. Suzuki and Conan Lee Hong Kong 1981

Leon Spinks and Ron in Russia

Ron Jr. at 6 years old

Zen Moment at All American 1998

Kai Van Clief at 5 ½ years old

THE BLACK DRAGON Philippines 1974

The Death of Bruce Lee

FIST OF FEAR TOUCH OF DEATH
Ron Van Clief and Bruce Lee

Hong Kong 1973 on the set
of *The Death of Bruce Lee*
270

My son Ron Jr. the best son anyone could ever have

Ron Van Clief and Ron Patel demonstrate aikijitsu for Warriors Magazine

Something I drew for my mom - circa 1953

**In front of 272 east 7th street homestead
Taimak, Mike and Ron circa 1981**

**My father, Allaire Van Clief
aka Larry**

The Squeeze aka *The Rip Off*

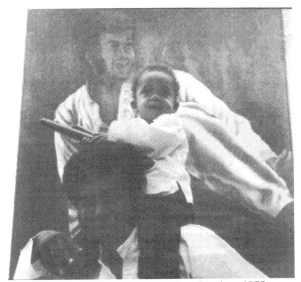

The Black Dragon and son Ron Jr. circa 1975

RICHIE HAVENS
My friend and martial arts brother
Thank you Richie for everything

LAURA VAN CLIEF
AERIALIST-STUNTWOMAN
MARTIAL ARTIST

A truly amazing aerialist and superwoman

My friend and teacher GM Chuck Merriman
Thank you for all the Zen lessons

My hero and mentor Kenny Hall at 77 years young
Truly an inspiration since I was trained by him in the 1950's

**Once a marine
Always a marine
Never Quit!**

24476777R00161

Made in the USA
San Bernardino, CA
25 September 2015